EMPOWER YOUR
SUCCESS SERIES
BY SCOTT ALLAN

You are enough
You are perfect
You can choose at every moment in time
You are loved.
God is with you

Empower Your **Gratitude**.

Your Free Gift

As a way of saying thanks for your purchase, I'm offering a free digital product that's exclusive to readers of the
Empowered Your Success Series:

The Fearless Confidence Action Guide: 17 Action Plans for Overcoming Fear and Increasing Confidence

To learn more, go to the link below and gain access right now:

https://scottallanauthor.com/fearless-confidence-action-guide/

https://scottallanauthor.com/fearless-confidence-action-guide/

Empower Your
Gratitude

*Overcome Your Scarcity Mindset and Build Limitless
Abundance with the Joy of Living and the Power of
Giving*

Scott Allan

ISBN Paperback: 978-1-989599-99-0
ISBN Hardcover: 978-1-989599-98-3
ISBN eBook: 978-1-989599-97-6

CONTENTS

The world has **enough** beautiful mountains and meadows, **spectacular** skies and serene lakes. It has enough lush forests, flowered fields, and sandy beaches. It has **plenty of** stars and the promise of a new sunrise and sunset every day. What the **world needs** more of is people to **appreciate** and **enjoy** it.

— Michael Josephson

Introduction

"Gratitude is a powerful catalyst for happiness. It's the spark that lights a fire of joy in your soul."

Amy Collette

NOTE TO MY READER: *If you take intentional action on what you shall learn from Empower Your Gratitude, the book you now have in your hands, it will herald you on a journey of transformative change and the life you've always wanted!*

Many of us often complain of the things we don't have in our lives, and all we think we ought to have, but don't because of this or that reason.

We complain, then complain some more, and follow it up with some more complaining. Eventually, because as Zig Ziglar once said, **repetition is the mother of learning and the father of action**, when we complain every chance we get, complaining becomes our attitude because, in the end, what we practice we eventually become.

This book is here to change all of that so that your life becomes beautiful than ever, and you turn into the finest version of yourself.

Empower Your Gratitude is a compilation of **40 impactful lessons** that illustrate the importance of gratitude. Furthermore, we'll focus on why integrating it in every facet of your life is in your best interest, and share actionable strategies you can use to start practicing gratitude in your everyday life.

The lessons are short, crisp, and easy to read, and therefore, you can quickly skim through them. Being easy to skim through does not mean what you'll learn won't be impactful in your life. If you read this book and ponder deeply on what you learn, the power of gratitude will help you make great personal discoveries.

Whether you choose to skim through the book, learning as you go, or contemplate every lesson, the only way you can benefit from this guide and harness the magic of gratitude is by consistently taking the action steps at the end of each lesson. Let me remind you that it's one thing to read the book and talk the talk, but only walking the walk can generate results in reality.

Therefore, to create the life of your dreams, please take intentional action on what you will learn from the material, and stay focused on your goal of being grateful.

With time and practicing gratitude consistently, you will notice a remarkable improvement in your life and substantial shifts in your emotions, thought process, and behavior. That's how powerful gratitude is.

Gratitude is medicine for the soul, and it is the cure for suffering, insecurity, worry and fear. Gratitude will, literally, change your life if you practice it

The Extraordinary Power of Gratitude

Gratitude is quite influential in a covert way. It does not give you huge muscles to fight or incredible stamina to run one marathon after the other. What it does is give you the strength to withstand obstacles, the courage to fight adversities, and the awareness to acknowledge your blessings.

Research shows that nurturing gratitude helps improve your emotional well-being, boost your resilience, reduce depression and stress, and strengthen your bond with loved ones.

The more grateful you are, the better your well-being and quality of life. You also have a fortified immune system, better sleeping habits, lower blood pressure, a lower likelihood of contracting life-threatening diseases, and a greater appreciation for your health and life.

Additionally, you tend to more compassionate, generous, forgiving, content, and happier.

The instant you nurture gratitude, you feel happy with whatever blessing you have in your present life. For instance, you may be complaining about not having a luxury car, but if you feel thankful for the minivan you have, you realize that many other people don't even have a bicycle they can ride to work.

Gratitude shifts your focus from what's absent to what's present in your life, something that allows you to start recognizing and acknowledging your blessings. This realization brings revolutionary changes in your life.

It is not just in theory. Science backs this up too.

The Science Behind Gratitude

The multinational company, Globoforce, believes that gratitude is the secret ingredient for developing a healthy and beneficial workplace culture.

In their award-winning book, *The Power of Thanks*, Eric Mosley and Derek Irvine, who is the CEO and VP of Globoforce, talk about the impact of being thankful in life and how gratitude happens to be a prime mover of productivity, prosperity, and joy in your life.

But where's the science behind gratitude?

Two of the most important neurotransmitters or chemicals in your body are **dopamine** and **serotonin**. Neuroscientists call these neurotransmitters 'endorphins' because they improve your mood and promote feelings of happiness, tranquility, enthusiasm, and confidence in your mind and body. Amongst the many things and activities that can boost their production is 'nurturing gratitude.'

Every time you express gratitude for anything good and positive in your life, or whenever you feel thankful for someone, your brain triggers the release of dopamine into your body. The hormone makes you feel good, which, in turn, makes you want more of it, and so, you continue to think happy thoughts, keep feeling positive, and focus on the good things in your life.

In addition, it promotes camaraderie and drives positive pro-social behaviors. As a result, you feel motivated, optimistic, and enthusiastic in life, find it easy to achieve goals, and stay happy.

Similarly, when you reflect on the positives related to your work and life, your brain commands the circulation of serotonin in your body. The neurotransmitter enhances your mood and has the same effects as an anti-depressant. Within a little while, you feel energized, shift your focus to what's good in your life, and feel calm.

Because you want to continue reaping the benefits of these two endorphins, one of the key things you must do is keep these gratitude circuits up and running. The more you practice gratitude, the more active these circuits become.

With time, the neural pathways, which are routes created by hormones and neurons, strengthen, and the practice becomes habitual. It then becomes easier for you to nurture gratitude at all times and focus more on the good and happy things in life.

Studies on the Power of Gratitude

Researchers conducted a study to observe the effects of gratitude. They divided the participants into three groups, and all of them received the same kind of counseling.

Additionally, the researchers asked members of the first group to write a letter of gratitude to someone once every week for the three weeks, which was the study's duration.

The second group needed to pen down their profound feelings related to negative life experiences in their letters. On the other hand, the third group served more as the control group: group members didn't have to write anything.

The results were astonishing.

The participants who wrote gratitude letters reported feeling mentally and emotionally more peaceful and happier than the group made of those who wrote down their negative feelings and those who did not engage in any letter-writing activity.

Results of the study

Gratitude exists, and the more you practice it, the better you feel about yourself and your life.

Gratitude is not only helpful for well-adjusted, emotionally healthy individuals; it's for everyone, particularly those struggling with mental health problems and the constant issue of fixating on the negatives in life. Moreover, practicing gratitude while receiving psychotherapy generates even better results than just doing the latter because combining both combines the power of the two strategies.

At this point in our journey together, you must have realized that gratitude is a powerful force and that it can help you live a serene life. That's good, however:

Gratitude is more like a muscle that you need to exercise to strengthen.

Exercising the Gratitude Habit

To build an athletic body, you have to work out regularly. The more you exercise your muscles, the stronger they become. Gratitude follows a similar fashion.

The more you practice it, the stronger the neural pathways in your brain become. When you practice something a fair number of times, its respective pathway becomes so strong that the practice shifts to autopilot mode.

The autopilot mode is what you use to drive your car now, swim in the pool, or do something else you have habitually practiced over time. Once something becomes wired in your mind to the extent that you can do it unconsciously, it moves to your brain's autopilot mode, and that's when it becomes a constant in your routine.

Given this, to feel more hopeful in the darkest of times and, when nothing seems right, to think positively, you need to exercise gratitude in the same manner.

Work it out every day and even multiple times during the day to ensure its corresponding neural pathways become etched in your mind. That's when you will discover something good in even the most dreadful situations, and that's how you will get the power and drive to move on.

This book will get you started on that path and be a faithful companion along the way as you turn yourself into a positively grateful individual.

What You Will Learn in This Book

As mentioned earlier, this book contains **40 lessons**, all of them centered on gratitude and the magnanimity and compassion it adds to your life.

The lessons are concise and precise, followed by actionable tips, so you can easily scan them and apply them in your daily routine.

Here is a small sampling of the impactful knowledge you will learn from this empowering book:

- The life-rewarding benefits of gratitude

- Life-changing effects of gratitude on your physical, emotional, and psychological health

- How to use the gratitude energy to manifest anything you want

- A clear understanding of the scarcity mindset and how to replace it with abundance

- Awareness of the gratitude opposites

- The importance of being mindful, how it helps you nurture gratitude, and how to achieve mindfulness in routine life

- How to use the healing power of gratitude

- Experiencing the massive power of giving

- Evils that destroy gratitude

- The right way to use gratitude to improve your work life, personal relationships, win over people, and build more social networks

- How to use gratitude to scale up your professional growth

- Using gratitude to achieve all your dreams and aspirations

As you learn these lessons, you'll find it easier to make room for gratitude in your life. Moreover, after some time, the ounce of gratitude you had turns into an overflowing river that spreads to every nook and corner of your life, engulfing everything in waves of serenity and contentment.

How to Use This Book

Empower Your Gratitude is a simple read. Instead of requiring you to read it in a chapter-by-chapter mannerism, it makes reading and learning easy for you.

Go through the list of contents, pick any chapter with the lessons that resonate with your state of mind, life, and the improvements you wish to bring forth, and read away. Pick a lesson that hits a chord with you, and start working on it.

If, however, you like to progress through a book in a step-by-step manner, start from the beginning, take your time with every chapter, and gradually move forward.

The best thing about this guide is that there is no way to read and utilize it. How you choose to gain from it is entirely on you. What matters is that you take the time to read it, in bits or as a whole, and practice what you learn in your life.

This book has one aim: to help you become grateful, optimistic, content, and happy. As long as you are implementing the strategies discussed in the book regularly, you will reap great rewards beyond all expectations. Better yet, the surrounding energy within your environment

One of the best ways to use this book is to pick a lesson, write it down, explore ways to incorporate it into your real life, and then, practice it for a couple of days and track your performance and progress. Then, slowly work on another lesson and keep moving forward in this manner.

In a matter of weeks, you will observe a spectrum of changes in your mindset, behavior, decision-making abilities, and state of life, and I assure you all of them will be positive.

As a reminder, this book has six core sections, each of which carries different chapters comprising various gratitude-based lessons. Therefore, based on your current needs, you can select a section or sub-category within a section and move straight into reading it instead of moving in an A to Z manner.

Empower Your Success Series

Additionally, remember to check out the entire Empower Your Success series for all available titles. You can actualize all your dreams and goals, take control of your mindset and govern your thoughts through the systems and training taught in each book.

As you work through each book in the series, you will be empowered with unbreakable confidence and action-focused strategies designed to get you the results you need. My **Empower Your Success Series** is created to provide you with the tools, resources and motivational tactics all epic performers need to continuously scale up and push forward.

You can access all available titles in this series here:

Scott Allan's Empower Your Success Series

Share This Book…Please!

Wisdom only grows when you share it with others. That applies to happiness and gratitude, too. Therefore, as you benefit from the philosophy of *Empower Your Gratitude*, I ask only one thing: Please share this with your friends and family, coworkers, bosses, neighbors, and everyone you meet on your journey.

I truly believe that gratitude is the medicine for developing better health, building relationships, and improving the quality all lives.

By expressing gratitude in your life with the world around you, you will play a part in helping people become more grateful and happier in life.

Your reward for living a life of gratitude is a stronger immune system, meaningful friendships, and waking up every morning with a sense of purpose and passion.

Your life is the greatest gift the universe has given you. Now let's dive into the material and discover all the ways the gift of gratitude can change your life.

Your attitude develops the gift of gratitude, and in the rest of this book, I will teach you everything you need to align attitude with abundance.

This is the place where dreams are made.

Let's make yours now!

Thankfulness is the **beginning** of gratitude. Gratitude is the completion of thankfulness. Thankfulness may consist merely of words. **Gratitude** is shown in acts.

— *Henri Frederic Amiel*

Section 1

The Many Benefits of Gratitude

"Nothing is more honorable than a grateful heart."

Lucius Annaeus Seneca

Introduction to Section 1: The Many Benefits of Gratitude

A grateful heart is a blessing that attracts many other countless blessings that make your life happy and well-rounded. When you strongly believe that what you have is sufficient and that you are also happy with it, you automatically feel it. That is because you need to believe in something to manifest it.

Similarly, to feel grateful, you must believe in it. Once you start doing that, you experience great joy in life.

Let us focus on integrating the power of gratitude, and its many benefits it brings into our lives.

Turn the page and let's begin.

Chapter 1: The Life-changing Benefits of Gratitude

"For my part, I am almost contented just now and very thankful. Gratitude is a divine emotion: it fills the heart, but not to bursting; it warms it, but not to fever."

Charlotte Bronte

Gratitude makes you notice the goodness all around you without blinding you to the harsh realities of life. It ensures that, when your life is more chaotic than ever, you get a good dose of positivity that ensures that you don't lose sight of the goodness and hope in life.

Let's walk through the life-changing effects of gratitude that inject meaning and tranquility into your life.

Ten Life-Changing Effects of Gratitude

#1: It reduces our need for greed

Acknowledging what you have and feeling grateful for it promotes contentment. You feel satisfied and happy with your blessings.

Instead of thinking about why you don't live in a mansion, you feel blessed to have a roof over your head. The more you practice gratitude, the more this sense of gratification increases, which gradually subsides your greed and the need to want more without any purpose.

#2: It helps you nurture empathy and generosity

As your need for more reduces and your level of contentment and thankfulness increases, you become aware of the plight and problems people around you go through. You develop a keen eye and a loving heart for the problems others experience, which turns you into an empathetic soul who is ready to share love and his/ her blessings with others.

Realizing that what you have is good enough opens your heart to nurture benevolence and generosity for others. "Sharing is caring" becomes your motto, and you turn into a kind soul who is ready to help people in need.

#3: It boosts your self-confidence

Seeing yourself become compassionate enough to be a helping hand to others, bring a smile on their faces, and be a source of comfort makes you feel good about yourself.

In addition, when you free yourself from constant complaining, you have more mental space to focus on the important tasks in life, which increases your productivity. You find yourself completing projects faster and boosting your productivity, which consequently boosts your confidence.

#4: Gratitude makes you optimistic and patient

It's near impossible to feel negative and thankful simultaneously. Once you let in gratitude in your life and habits, it expands to make room for other positive emotions such as appreciation, joy, patience, and hope. It gives you the courage to ignore the negatives of a situation, so you start to analyze the positives.

You understand how things won't always remain unfortunate, and good days too will come. You gain the stamina to wait for the desired outcomes while optimistically working for them.

A study shows that maintaining a weekly gratitude journal results in a 5% increase in positivity. Another study shows how keeping the same journal daily skyrockets your optimism by 15%.

#5: It promotes feelings of security

A thankful attitude helps you place your faith in the power of the universe and the greater good in the world.

You find better things coming your way once you start to believe in the power of gratitude and genuinely nurture gratitude for what you have. That helps you realize how the universe is on your side, and you feel secure and connected to it.

#6: Gratitude fosters love and happiness in relationships

With a heart full of warmth and love, you find it easier to spread joy with everyone. So many of our problems in life result from nurturing a complaining attitude that also makes us irritable towards loved ones.

Once the whining gets replaced with acknowledgment and appreciation, you become kinder, patient, warmer, and loving with dear ones, which helps mend strained relationships. When loved ones surround you, your life automatically becomes happier.

#7: It can help save your marriage

Quite often, marriages suffer when the passion fizzles. That's when the partners nag each other more and acknowledge each other's good qualities less.

Scientists have developed an 'appreciation to nagging' ratio called the Losada ratio. The best way to derive this ratio is by dividing the total number of positive expressions such as appreciation, encouragement, and support during a typical interaction over the negative expressions such as cynicism, sarcasm, and disapproval.

Different studies have tried to check and confirm this ratio. When this ratio is lower than 0.9, there were 11% more negative expressions and gestures than the positive ones, which ultimately made the marriages plummet towards languishment and even divorce. On the other hand, all the marriages where the positivity ratio was over 5.1 lasted longer, and the respective partners had a more satisfactory relationship.

If you are experiencing marital problems or relationship issues with your spouse, build a habit of being thankful for one another and the joys you get to celebrate every single day. The more you cultivate gratitude, the better the chances of your relationship going long and strong.

#8: Gratitude reduces materialism

Materialism often causes high rates of mental health problems and an overall reduced state of well-being. There is nothing wrong with wanting and having more.

However, quite often, a materialistic attitude increases your greed for material gains. This increase makes you focus more on what you don't have, reduces your ability to appreciate little joys in life, makes you compare yourself more to others, and also increases feelings of self-centeredness.

Many studies have shown that increased power and wealth reduce your happiness and well-being. In trying to have more, you often make great sacrifices, spend less time with family, and become status conscious.

Additionally, at other times, you fixate on just being wealthy instead of fulfilling goals that truly matter to you. All of this affects your emotional and mental state of well-being, which lowers your quality of life.

On the other hand, a grateful heart makes you worry less about the materialistic gains and wins in life.

#9: Gratitude enhances your connection to the universe

With gratitude, spirituality transcends your life. Spiritual leaders often revere gratitude as an important virtue because it brings forth peace and acceptance in your life.

It helps you make your peace with all your woes, accept your life as it is, and use that sense of gratification to explore a clearer direction in life, which gradually unlocks and increases your spirituality.

#10: Aligns you with mindfulness

Mindfulness is a state of mind and awareness that makes you live in the moment, worry less about the past, accept it as a bygone, not fret about the future since it is uncertain, but embrace whatever comes at the moment without judging it or holding any ill feelings against it.

With an increased state of mindfulness, you hold on to the moment, focus better on it, and enjoy it to the maximum.

You also experience a massive relief from stress and worries because you bother less about the 'what ifs,' 'buts,' and 'things that have had happened.' Being free from all this improves your overall productivity, which helps you achieve better outcomes in every aspect of life.

Additionally, when you're mindfully grateful, you focus more on improving instead of what went wrong. That allows you to use your time, energy, and resources at hand to the best of your abilities.

Moreover, when you stop judging and labeling things as 'good' or 'bad' and 'right' or 'wrong,' you become receptive to your emotions, explore different options, and become open to the idea of experimenting in life.

This sense of awareness and self-discovery leads to great findings, allowing you to pursue the most meaningful endeavors in life, thus making your life more worthwhile than ever.

Has all this motivated you enough to start building gratitude? Let me encourage you some more by highlighting the health benefits of gratitude in the following chapter.

"Gratitude rewards generosity and maintains the cycle of healthy social behavior.

Antonia Damasio

Chapter 2: The Mental and Physical Health Benefits of Gratitude

"If you concentrate on finding whatever is good in every situation, you will discover that your life will suddenly be filled with gratitude, a feeling that nurtures the soul."

Rabbi Harold Kushner

Thankfulness improves every imaginable aspect of your life—and no, that's not an overstatement: Gratitude is the medicine for creating long-term happiness.

Now that we have discussed how gratitude impacts different areas of your personal and professional life, spirituality, and relationships, let me walk you through the different ways it improves your physical and mental health.

The Physical and Mental Health Impact of Gratitude

#1: It reduces stress, anxiety, and depression.

We stress and worry about things beyond our control, bygones, and the constant worries of the future. Gratitude helps cultivate mindfulness, which automatically lets you let go of all these issues, thereby soothing stress and anxiety.

Danielle Cripps—a researcher—mentions how gratitude diary intervention in school helps alleviate anxiety. Yes, gratitude alone won't help you overcome anxious thoughts, but it certainly plays a big role because it shifts your focus from what may happen to what is now, which helps you foster peace and harmony in the present.

Moreover, gratitude also reduces depression, helping you take a break-free from it. Feelings of dejection and disappointment are the primary cause of depression. On the other hand, gratitude makes you aware of your blessings, which improves your feelings of despair and soothes your depression.

Nurturing gratitude also activates your parasympathetic nervous system, which lowers circulating stress hormones such as cortisol and promotes relaxation in the body, which automatically reduces your stress and tensions.

#2: It controls overthinking.

Setbacks trigger frustration, persistent worry, and ongoing stress, which increases your tendency to engage in overthinking. According to a German study conducted in 2019, gratitude can control negative thoughts that lead to overthinking.

These researchers proved that nurturing gratitude helps one manage toxic thoughts that make us obsess with doubts, fears, and insecurities and lead to negative outcomes.

#3: It declutters Mind.

Our mind is usually jumping from one branch of thought to another, which is why we rush from one task to another, focus poorly on tasks, and feel chaotic from within.

Gratitude and mindfulness help us focus on the here and now, which gives us a break from the constant stream of thoughts and helps us focus on one thought and task at a time.

Also, when we experience reduced stress, anxiety, and worries and experience an increased level of self-discovery, we experience a decluttered state of mind that breathes peace in our life.

#4: Helps you sleep better.

Gratitude has also proven that it can reduce insomnia and improve sleep quality. Incessant worries, whether related to your kids, work, relationships, health, wealth, or other issues, are the main causes of poor quality and insufficient sleep. When you are grateful, you have fewer problems to worry about, which automatically enables you to sleep comfortably at night.

In a study of 65 participants with chronic pain issues, researchers noticed that those who worked on their daily gratitude journal slept better and for half an hour longer than those who did not engage in the activity. Another study of 400 people shows that those scoring better on gratitude tests slept better.

Thinking about all the things you're grateful for improves your quality of sleep. Gratitude promotes positive thinking and reduces worry and anxiety. For sleep, this is critical in getting a deep and well-rested sleep.

In their seminal research, psychologists Robert Emmons and Michael McCullough asked people with neuromuscular disorders to make nightly lists of things for which they were grateful. After several weeks, participants reported getting longer, more refreshing sleep.

By cultivating and consistently practicing gratitude throughout your day, you're building the mind-body experience to have a good sleep.

#5: Improves heart and brain health.

Paul J. Mills, Ph.D. and a professor at the University of California in San Diego, and his colleagues conducted studies to gauge the effect of gratitude on cardiovascular health. The research study, later published by the American Psychological Association, discovered that being grateful improved heart health in patients with risks of experiencing heart failure.

As shown by different research studies, gratitude also enhances your psychological well-being and your brain health.

Researchers working at the University of Southern California's (USC) Brain and Creativity Institute aspired to see how gratitude changes brain chemistry. They used the personal stories of various Holocaust survivors as the research tool.

The researchers recruited 23 volunteers in their 20's with no link to the Holocaust. They watched and listened to documentaries regarding the Holocaust survivors recalling their experiences. Some survivors reported getting shelter, clothing, and food from strangers and feeling grateful for receiving that help.

Dr. Paul and his colleagues also asked the study participants to imagine that they were amongst those oppressed during the Holocaust and the feelings they would experience if someone offered them the same help the actual victims went through. While the volunteers visualized this scenario, the research team took MRI scans of their brains.

The results revealed that nurturing gratitude stimulated the brain regions—the anterior cingulate cortex and pre-frontal cortex—in charge of producing feelings of moral cognition, fairness, and reward.

#6: Strengthens the immune system and improves overall health

Gratitude can improve your mental and psychological health, which consequently affects your overall health. This is more than a theory; more than <u>137 research studies</u> have proven it true.

These studies have shown that gratitude has positive effects such as management and coping with terminal health problems such as HIV and cancer, better recovery from medical procedures, fortified immune system, and healthier behavior.

Scientific research also shows that people who engage in regular gratitude-based practices experience less pain, have fewer doctor visits, fewer complaints of hypertension (high blood pressure), and a lower likelihood of developing mental disorders.

#7: Helps Build Laser Focus

Gratitude can also help you build laser focus and resilience in life. A study conducted on 110 college students examined these effects.

Fifty of those students received constant reminders throughout the day to practice gratitude and relevant exercises. They received these reminders through text messages sent 4 to 5 days every week for three whole months. The control group in the study consisted of 60 students who did not receive any such reminders.

Compared to the control group, the results revealed that those who received the regular gratitude reminders had increased focus in lessons and could concentrate better on tasks at hand.

#8: Increases lifespan

Yes, gratitude is not like a magical potion that makes you immortal; however, it can still help you live longer. "How," you may ask.

Well, so far, you have seen how gratefulness improves heart health, immune system and how it fortifies your overall health. Therefore, naturally, when you develop coping mechanisms against diseases, stay happier and stress-free, and sleep better, your emotional and physical health improves, which improves your longevity.

Moreover, different studies have shown that optimistic people tend to live a couple of years longer than pessimistic people. We can attribute this to the fact that optimism broadens your horizon, whereas pessimism narrows it.

With a narrow vision, you easily surrender to difficulties in life instead of finding solutions; you find yourself flooded with mental and physical health issues that affect your longevity.

#9: Boosts your energy levels

It may surprise you to learn that gratitude and vitality have a solid relationship. Different research studies conducted over the years have shown that.

For example, one study that involved 238 people discovered a direct correlation between gratefulness and vitality, thereby showing that the two have a very close relationship. While researchers are yet to figure out the reasons behind it, it is quite likely that this effect stems from how gratitude helps you sleep better, focus on important things, and how it improves your overall health.

Your energy levels drop when stress engulfs you. It also engulfs you when you have countless worries to fret about, toss and turn throughout the night, have low productivity, feel grumpy, and constantly struggle with mental and physical health issues. These issues slowly get resolved, you feel enthusiastic and energetic.

Moreover, also note that gratitude improves the levels of the endorphins: dopamine and serotonin. Both these neurotransmitters play a key role in your confidence and enthusiasm. Hence, with more of these happy hormones circulating in your body, you feel joyful and vigorous.

#10: Encourages you to exercise more

Here is another incredible benefit of gratitude you may not have heard of before. Yes, the caption is correct: gratitude can motivate you to exercise regularly.

In a study that involved 96 Americans, researchers observed that those who maintained a weekly gratitude journal successfully exercised 40 more minutes every week than the control group participants.

Although the researchers did not narrow down to the reasons for these results, if you access all the benefits of gratitude we have looked at so far, you will see the close association between gratitude and the likelihood of exercising more.

With better sleep patterns, improved mental health, and increased clarity, you find it easier to pay attention to the important things in life, including your health, making it easier to make healthier decisions.

Gratitude makes you conscious of your good health and helps you recognize it as a key blessing. This realization encourages you to take better care of yourself and stimulates you to adopt measures to achieve better health, including exercising regularly.

All in all, the more grateful and optimistic you feel, the easier you find it to sustain the habit of exercising regularly, which automatically improves your overall health.

As you can see, gratitude is a true blessing. Given everything we have discussed so far, I am sure that the positive benefits of gratitude have won you over and motivated you to get started with your gratitude journey.

You want to become happy, enthusiastic, confident, healthy, and stress-free, don't you? Well, you can achieve all of that and a lot more by making gratitude a daily, all-permeating habit.

Are you excited to learn how you can make that happen?

Let us kick start this journey by practicing the different habits in the chapters that follow.

"Gratitude turns what we have into enough and more. It turns denial into acceptance, chaos into order, confusion into clarity...it makes sense of our past, brings peace for today, and creates a vision for tomorrow."

Melody Beattie

Chapter 3: Manifest Anything You Want with the "Gratitude Energy"

"Let us rise up and be thankful, for if we didn't learn a lot today, at least we learned a little, and if we didn't learn a little, at least we didn't get sick, and if we got sick, at least we didn't die; so, let us all be thankful."

Buddha

If we start being thankful for just a few of our blessings, life will become ever so serene. Gratitude has beautiful, calming energy. You may not realize it right now, but when you start practicing it, you will become aware of its power and be in a position to harness it too.

Before diving into the gratitude energy, I encourage you to quickly take a little test to find out how grateful you are right now—or up to this point in your life.

Take the Gratitude Test: How Grateful Are You?

Are you thankful for the good things in life bestowed upon you, or are you amongst those who take those blessings for granted?

Research has repeatedly proven that grateful people are the happiest. Given this, it's important to find out how thankful you are in reality. Here is a quick and simple test that can help you determined that. Based on a scale created by renowned psychologists Nancy Fagley and Mitchel Adler, this gratitude test quickly gives you an idea of where you stand on the gratitude spectrum.

You can use the following link to access the test:

https://greatergood.berkeley.edu/quizzes/take_quiz/gratitude

Once you take the test, you will get a score out of 105. Those with scores of 90 to 105 have very high gratitude levels; those with scores lying between 70 to 89 have moderate to high gratitude levels, and those with scores below that need to work on it a bit.

The test will also assess your gratitude level; this assessment helps you better comprehend your state of gratefulness and further work on it. Once you take the test and realize you are struggling with being grateful, do not worry about it at all because this is what this guide is for: *to help you become more grateful and happier.*

From the moment you take the test, commit to nurturing the gratitude energy to improve your gratitude level.

Understanding Gratitude Energy

Every emotion, feeling, thought, inanimate object, living being, and every single thing in the universe have energy as its core constituent. Since energy is vibratory, so is everything made up of it. Based on its vibrations, different things have different frequencies and give off different vibes.

Gratitude possesses incredibly massive energy that exudes light. Its positive energy warms up your heart and opens it to receive the many good things the universe has to offer you.

When energy moves around, it draws towards itself things with similar energy, and that's how it allows you to manifest your desires into reality. With gratitude in your heart, mind, and soul, you hold gratitude energy and all its glory.

This energy becomes the essence of your thoughts, ideas, spirit, and the vibes you exude. When you think or do anything, you give off this gratitude energy that travels far and wide, drawing towards your brilliant things.

That's how you materialize all your desires and turn them into reality.

That's when **nothing remains impossible for you**.

That's when you become the creator of all things positive in your life because you brim with gratitude.

Make Gratitude Your #1 Choice of the Day

To allow the gratitude energy to take over you and become your reality, you need to put some effort into adopting. Fortunately, doing that is rather simple. All you need to do is to make gratitude your #1 and only choice of the day.

You may not realize this right now, but if you take a closer look at things, you will realize that you have a choice in everything you do: from choosing what to wear, eat, where to go, which design tool to use: you have a selection to pick from in every aspect of your life.

Similarly, when it comes to gratitude, it is solely your choice to make, and you can opt for it easily by following the steps below:

1. **Start your day on the gratitude note:** How you feel when you wake up sets your mood for the day. If you reset your mood and tone at that very point, you are likely to have quite a positive day ahead irrespective of the mishaps that may come your way.

    Therefore, when you wake up, even if you feel a tad bit cranky or couldn't sleep well through the night, be grateful for one thing. Feel happy about waking up, or for seeing the sun bright and shiny after days of downpour, or for having your family next to you.

    Acknowledge anything in your life right now, and say, ***"I am thankful for (name the blessing), and this feeling makes me happy."*** Chant it in your head or out loud a couple of times and let the warm feeling of contentment dance on your face.

2. **Keep practicing the gratitude mantra:** Since you have to choose gratitude, look for something to be grateful about throughout the day. When you shower, be thankful for having enough water to clean yourself while many other people don't have enough water to drink.

    When you dress up, be happy for fresh clothes to wear. When sitting down to eat, express your gratitude for having warm food to consume. When attending a call from your friend, be thankful for having at least a phone even though it isn't the latest model.

Every time you pay your gratitude for something, clearly say, *"I am thankful for (name the blessing), and this feeling makes me happy."*

3. **Keep choosing gratitude:** Set reminders on your phone to constantly choose gratitude in every situation. Whether your boss just called you in for an urgent meeting, or your colleague called in sick, piling more work on your shoulders, be thankful for having a job, a means to earn income, and opportunities to shine and show your worth to your boss and coworkers.

    When you practice gratitude in every situation, it becomes your go-to mechanism, making you feel positive throughout the day.

4. **Journal your blessings:** When the day ends, write down all the blessings you counted so far in your journal. It is a good idea to jot down bullet points of a blessing the instant you acknowledge it; that way, you don't have to shake your memory much to recall your gifts of the day.

Action Step: Create an attitude of gratitude

Practice the four steps discussed above every single day. Set reminders and leave little notes in different places of your house, such as in your shower, on your bathroom mirror, on your nightstand, on your closet door, etc., to remind yourself to choose gratitude at every moment of your day.

Before you realize it, you will have developed the attitude of gratitude, and thankfulness will become your settled mannerism of thinking and feeling. For example, whether you get stuck in a traffic jam, haven't slept the night, or incur a business loss, you will find something to be thankful for in that difficult situation and find a way out of it.

Just try this practice right now.

Be thankful for one thing, from having the ability to hold a pen to affording a laptop to having friends around: acknowledge your blessings and see how great you feel within minutes.

With this attitude, keep moving forward and continue empowering your gratitude as you use this book to the best of your abilities.

"This is a wonderful day. I've never seen this one before."

Maya Angelou

I truly believe we can either see the **connections**, celebrate them, and **express gratitude** for our **blessings**, or we can see life as a string of coincidences that have no meaning or connection. For me, I'm going to believe in **miracles**, celebrate life, **rejoice** in the views of **eternity**, and hope my choices will create a **positive ripple effect** in the lives of others. This is my **choice**."

— *Mike Ericksen*

Section 2

Gratitude and Abundance

"When you are grateful, fear disappears, and abundance appears.

— *Anthony Robbins*

Introduction to Section 2: Gratitude and Abundance

Abundance comes from the word 'abundantia,' which is of Latin origin. It means "to have something in plenty" and is the natural tendency of life and nature to grow and multiply.

The life force is multiplicative, which means it produces more of everything. That is why we often have new stars in the galaxy, new trees in the forests, new fruit species coming up, and growth everywhere.

Growth is part of the universe or cosmos, and thus, because everything is part of the cosmos, growth is the destiny of everything, us (humans) included. That calls to mind a fundamental question:

If it's our destiny to grow spiritually, personally, professionally, and even in terms of progeny, why do so many of us feel stuck?

Why do so many of us struggle to grow better?

Why is it challenging for some of us to manifest abundance and truly experience it?

What keeps us from being abundant?

A closer observation of the issue reveals that gratitude could be the missing link in the equation.

Chapter 4: The Connection Between Gratitude and Abundance

"Gratitude will shift you to a higher frequency, and you will attract much better things."

Rhonda Byrne

Most of us don't realize that we already have what we desire deeply, be it inner freedom, love, connection, etc. We need to realize this more so we can undertake it all with a sense of complete abundance. Our inner abundance exudes ease, value, and love, which all find roots in gratitude.

5 Ways Gratitude Creates Abundance

With no abundance in life, we can be around riches and still feel lost and poor. Only by realizing that we have enough can we recognize and acknowledge our abundance and manifest true happiness.

Here are the five ways gratitude creates abundance in your life.

1. **It helps you realize you have enough:** When you are grateful for little things in life, you realize you have enough. You feel thankful for having some bread and a pair of shoes to wear for the entire year because at least you have that instead of having nothing.

2. **It raises your vibrational frequency:** Gratitude has a high vibrational frequency. And so, by nurturing it, you raise yours too. With positive vibrations, you attract bigger, better things and manifest abundance in life.

3. **It makes you appreciative of people and things:** Thankfulness makes you appreciative of the bright crescent of the moon, your kid's unstoppable laughter, celebrating your promotion over a one piece of cake with friends, and the many joys in everyday moments that you may have missed. The more

you appreciate, the more positives vibes you radiate, which creates more abundance in your life.

4. **You work hard:** With gratitude comes contentment and positivity. You know you have enough, so instead of complaining, you use your available resources to achieve your goals. And by taking positive actions, you successfully create abundance for yourself.

5. **It helps you nurture an attitude of giving:** The gratitude attitude enables you to focus more on giving to others to spread joy around. By doing so, you follow the giving nature of the universe, which encourages it to send bounties towards you, hence creating more abundance in your life.

Gratitude brings about abundance, which ultimately leads to more prosperity.

To continue our learning journey, let us no turn our attention to the gratitude traits—or the abundant mindset—so you can know how to start developing one.

7 Traits of the Gratitude-Abundant Mindset

To attract abundance in life, nurturing an abundant mindset is crucial. The mindset of gratitude is a mindset of abundance. If you work on the following traits, you too can nurture this mindset:

1. **Express gratitude daily:** Grateful people who have an abundant mindset express their gratitude to the universe for their blessings daily. To build an abundant mindset, be thankful for what you have and express it openly every day.

2. **Focus on doing what they love:** Those with an abundance mentality spend more time doing things they love in preparation for and leverage bigger opportunities. To create more abundance, you should do the same. Find what you love and invest your time and energy into it to ensure the resultant positivity spreads far and wide, bringing desired goals your way.

3. **Spend time with grateful people:** People with an abundant mindset spend more time with other people who nurture the same mentality. That way, they learn from each other's experiences and inspire one another to do the same. Thus, identify people in your social circle with an abundance mentality and slowly make more room for them by eliminating those with the scarcity mindset.

4. **Focus on your unique strengths:** Each of us has a unique capability that we need to explore, hone, and utilize to unleash our true potential. When we do that, we follow our path, which allows us to attract better and bigger opportunities. It's in your best interest to spend some time discovering your unique strengths so you can then use them positively to realize your meaningful goals and achieve them.

5. **Have clarity and live in the moment:** To build an abundant life, you must form a vision of how you want your future to look. Abundant people do the same by figuring out what they want, creating clear goals centered on those aspirations, and living in the moment to manifest the lives of their dreams gradually. Spend some time daily trying to understand your genuine ambitions and dreams.

    Next, ask yourself what you truly want to achieve in life, then create a goal around it. Train yourself to live in the moment by being thankful for it; that way, you can better focus on your dreams. Start with having a clear vision that ensures you don't feel confused about what you want.

6. **Create abundance around:** Accomplished people who have an abundant mentality don't just know what they want; they also strive for it. Once they get the clarity, they craft a plan to achieve it and then work on it diligently and consistently. That's the right way to materialize your goals and dreams, and it is time you start working on the same guidelines.

7. **Are energized and inspirational:** Abundant and grateful people don't just look out for themselves; they also look out for others. Because they are of positive energy, they are always

inspiring others to do better. So, start nurturing more positive, happy thoughts because the more you think positive, the more positive energy you will radiate and inspire others to be the same.

At first, working on these guidelines will not be easy. However, once you get started, you will realize that getting started is usually all it takes to bring about impactful change in your life.

Once you start practicing these traits as part of your personality, there will be no going back, and that's how you will channelize the LOA's power.

"If the only prayer you said in your whole life was "thank you" that would suffice."

Meister Eckhart

Chapter 5: Gratitude and The Law of Attraction

"Be thankful for what you have; you'll end up having more. If you concentrate on what you don't have, you will never, ever have enough."

Oprah Winfrey

If you think about Oprah Winfrey's quote above for even a minute, you will realize it alludes to the "law of attraction," aka LOA, a law rooted in the simple universal rule of *"like attracts like."*

What you think, you become, and the thoughts you send out manifest your reality. That is why a complaining attitude and failing to acknowledge your blessings never leads to abundance. To harness the mighty force of the LOA, nurturing gratitude is a MUST.

Focusing on The Law of Attraction

From our discussion in the last chapter, you know we are energy beings, vibrating energy at all times. This energy goes out in the universe, which on receiving those vibrations, sends us exactly what it receives. Therefore, what we get is a reflection of what we send into the universe.

Your emotions play a monumental role in this equation because they affect your thought process and behavior pattern. If you feel positive, you radiate positive energy. On the other hand, when negative thoughts lurk in your mind, negativity is what you exude.

Gratitude is a strong virtue that brings about emotional satisfaction, pleasure, joy, and trust. Harboring these emotions raises your vibrational energy. When your vibrational energy is high, you transmit more positivity to the universe. The universe receives and then sends similar positive experiences towards you.

Every thought and emotion has some related experiences. When they interact with other thoughts and emotions in the universe, they draw the experiences tied to them towards them as well. That is why you attract happy experiences when you are happy and undesirable experiences when you are upset.

How Gratitude Helps You Tap into the Power of the LOA

"If the only prayer you said in your whole life was 'thank you,' that would suffice."

Meister Eckhart

Quite often, when trying to leverage the LOA, people forget to nurture gratitude.

We get so wrapped up in making lists and visualizing achieving our aims, goals, and dreams that we ignore one of the easiest and crucial aspects of the LOA: nurturing gratitude.

We see people living wonderful lives and others who only want those things but cannot achieve them. What the latter is missing from their lives is gratitude.

The latter's inability to practice gratitude keeps them from receiving the goodness the universe has to offer. Instead, because they focus more on complaining, they send complaints and rants to the universe, which is what the universe sends to them in exchange.

Understand that the universe does not focus on problems or even recognize them. Instead, everything in the universe complements the creative energy within us, and thus, we are responsible for creating our problems and opportunities.

Thus, to experience more goodness in your life, you need to send goodness out too, and that's what gratitude allows you to do with ease. Gratitude reminds you of your many blessings, thereby helps you cultivate contentment. The universe receives your contentment, joy, and pleasure, marries them to other similar emotions and experiences, and sends the same your way.

I Own Nothing but Have Everything

To use gratitude to channelize the LOA, you need to embrace the important rule of abundance: *"I own nothing but have everything."*

Everywhere you look, you find abundance. You can manifest the same abundance in your life by accepting and exercising the notion that you have everything but do not own it—at least not really. This mindset allows you to accept it as a part of the universe and feel it as your own, but without becoming attached to things.

When owning something comes into the equation, you also let go of the desire to share it with others. You become greedy and envious and want complete control of it without sharing it with others. The universe receives the ill sentiments and sends ill experiences your way.

Hence to use LOA the right way, you must understand and practice this rule. Here's what you need to do:

- Acknowledge your blessings and talk about them openly.

- Think about the value those blessings add to your life.

- Express your gratefulness to the universe for those blessings by repeating chants like, "I am thankful to the universe for my good job, loving kids, etc."

- Remind yourself that these blessings come from the universe.

- Think of the different treasures in the universe and how you can access all of them without owning them.

- Close your eyes and imagine yourself sitting in a beautiful valley with waterfalls and trees laden with delicious fruit. Think of different luxuries in life and how they pop up in front of you as you envisage them. You can use whatever you want as long as you remember that you can't keep it with you forever.

- In that visualization, add more people in and picture all of them living harmoniously with one another.

Practice this exercise daily, and you will soon accept how you have everything without owning it, be thankful for it, and use that power to bring better things your way.

If you want to achieve enhanced results faster, it is imperative to eliminate the scarcity mindset. You may think you don't have it, but only by studying it better can you make that distinction.

"So much has been given to me; I have no time to ponder over that which has been denied."

Helen Keller

Chapter 6: The Power of Giving

"Gratitude is riches. Complaint is poverty.

Doris Day

Abundance comes from practicing gratitude and understanding the power of giving. You may believe you are grateful, but only by understanding the power of giving and focusing on what you have can you exercise the true essence of gratitude and focus on being abundant in real life.

The Influence of Giving and Receiving Gratitude

To materialize the power of giving, you need to start with comprehending the influence of both giving and receiving gratitude.

When you give gratitude, you become capable of receiving it too. Giving may seem like a big thing to do right now, but it is quite simple to practice. All it takes to give and receive is a compassionate, grateful heart. Additionally, we often perceive giving as giving money; however, it does not always have to be in that sense.

Here's how you can start giving gratitude to receive it:

- Compliment loved ones for their qualities. For example, if your best friend is caring, let him know how much you appreciate that. If your partner has gorgeous hair, compliment her beautiful locks.

  Putting a smile on someone's face by making them feel good is a great way to give gratitude and appreciation to others, which encourages them to do the same to you, and that is when you receive gratitude.

- Be thankful to loved ones for being around and helping you in times of need. The more you are grateful to them, the more gratitude vibes you send into the universe.

- Be grateful for things like having rain after a long time, seeing the first snow of the winter season, having blooms in your garden, and so on.

- Practice small gestures of showing your gratefulness to others. For example, if you don't always verbally say thanks to your partner for helping you with household chores, gestures like making a special dinner for her or sending her flowers at work are also ways to express your gratitude to her.

It is a good practice to note down these gestures and practices as you engage in them in your journal; that way, you will track the measures and exercise them regularly to allow abundance to flow in your life.

Focus on What You Have

The absence of the right sense of focus seems to be a big obstacle while manifesting abundance. We get so occupied with whimpering about what we don't have that we fail to notice the many blessings in our lives.

A bleating attitude is that of scarcity, and while I will elaborate on it in detail in the following section, it is important to mention here what a lack of positive focus does to us.

For a moment, think that you will never be successful in life. Then, concentrate on it for a few moments until you start hearing thoughts and emotions of a similar pattern in your head.

You will start to recall your failures and mistakes and honestly believe you will amount to nothing but failure in life. Plus, you will also become more conscious of what you don't have: a six-figure salary, the love of your life, a happy family, the latest iPhone, a luxury car, and so on.

That is something most of us go through and what we need to change.

Fixing your sense of focus is crucial, and here is what you must do to get started on this process:

- Start being conscious of your thoughts. While we may say we know what we think and how the thoughts affect us, that may not always be the truth. We have about 50,000 to 70,000 thoughts a day, so it is likely to lose track of them.

  To be fully conscious of them, write them down. Well, you cannot jot down all of those, but you can start with the major ones or the ones that seem to rattle a lot in your head.

- When you have a meal, notice the first thought you have. Is it something that shows gratitude and contentment or has a more complaining undertone? When you leave for work on a subway, do you feel grateful for at least having the means to commute and being able to afford a subway ticket, or do you constantly grumble about why you don't have a personal car yet?

- Note down these thoughts and go through them. You will soon realize a pattern. If you tend to want more often, complain about what you have, or desire for what you want without acknowledging what is currently available, you are a little away from being grateful right now.

  However, that does not mean you can't be more grateful; you can. If you keep practicing the gratitude exercises in this guide, you will soon get there.

- When you notice that you don't fully acknowledge your blessings at hand, think about the value brought into your life by whatever you have. If you are wailing about having a studio apartment instead of a big home, think of what would happen if you don't have this roof over your head too.

  What then? What happens if you lose your job that you are always grumbling about and saying how much you hate? Think of how your life would look if you didn't have any water to drink?

- You will instantly find yourself feeling better about your current life. Write down those grateful thoughts.

- Once again, go through your current situation, whether you are eating, showering, or driving to work, and think of how you feel about what you have. The odds are high that thankfulness will have replaced your whining.

- Take a moment to acknowledge that feeling and blessing, expressing your gratitude to that blessing and the universe.

- Chant a gratitude-based affirmation such as, "I am grateful for this blessing," or "I am happy with what I have right now," about ten times out loud.

- It is best to write down that blessing; that way, you will have an extensive list of your gifts to go through every time you feel demotivated and ungrateful.

If you practice this exercise several times during the day, soon enough, it will become habitual. It will be on autopilot mode, and you'll find yourself paying thanks for your blessings throughout the day.

As you keep up with this practice, you will feel content with yourself and your life. You shall also start noticing notice abundance coming in your life through many different avenues.

Your next step is to get rid of the scarcity mindset that often hinders your growth. The next section primarily focuses on that.

"Stop now. Enjoy the moment. It's now or never."

Maxime Lagacé

Forget **yesterday**—it has already forgotten you. Don't sweat **tomorrow**—you haven't even met. Instead, open your eyes and your **heart** to a truly **precious** gift—today.

— *Steve Maraboli*

Section 3

Gratitude and Scarcity Mindset

"I looked around and thought about my life. I felt grateful. I noticed every detail. That is the key to time travel. You can only move if you are actually in the moment. You have to be where you are to get where you need to go."

Amy Poehler

Introduction to Section 3: Gratitude and Scarcity Mindset

We have talked a great deal about abundance and gratitude, and by now, you know why nurturing an abundance mindset is paramount to being grateful and manifesting your desired reality.

There are two main mindsets: the growth and fixed mindsets, often also called the abundance and scarcity/poverty mindsets, respectively.

The abundant or growth mindset, as the name suggests, focuses on growing and prospering. When you nurture this mindset, you believe you have unlimited growth and potential and can have access to and accomplish whatever you want.

In contrast, a poverty/scarcity/fixed mindset, whatever you may call it, suggests the opposite. Instead of focusing on creating abundance, it fixates on the negatives. Because it's rooted in your fears and negative thoughts, this mindset makes you believe that you can never have enough of anything, and you can never grow to your desired point of success.

It's easy to think that this stems from not having enough. However, in reality, it boils down to a lack of gratitude. This section will explore the relationship between a scarcity mindset and gratitude and how to improve on it.

Chapter 7: How Scarcity Mindset Ruins Your Life

"There is a calmness to a life lived in gratitude, a quiet joy."

Ralph H. Blum

To many, the scarcity mindset may seem like nothing more than a set of beliefs. However, the reality of the matter is that it has drastic repercussions that seriously affect the quality of your life.

If you often worry about how your efforts pertinent to your growth end up in vain and how even after years of hard work, you don't get the desired results, chances are you nurture a scarcity mindset.

What *is* a Scarcity Mindset?

Contrary to popular belief, poverty and scarcity is more than a state of mind; they are a belief system. Some rich people nurture a scarcity mindset, and seemingly poor people with a rich mindset. Having a scarcity mindset does not necessarily mean your bank account is empty too.

Your mindset is the set of beliefs, ideologies, and viewpoints you place your faith in and exercise to shape your life a certain way. Yes, most people with a scarcity mindset are financially poor, but that is not always the case.

A scarcity mindset makes you believe that your potential has a limit or limitation. And so, because you think you have fixed potential, you also think that you can only grow to a certain extent or experience a certain amount of success. No matter what you do, you cannot be rich and abundant because for that to happen, you need unlimited resources.

When you have this mindset, you struggle to accomplish your goals and achieve your desired success. That's because your focus is usually on how limited you are and, therefore, how undeserving you are.

What's the actual problem?

Those with a poverty mindset may blame their lack of resources or unfortunate destiny for their lack of success.

However, in reality, it's because the scarcity mindset is a deeply rooted lack of gratitude.

Think about it.

When do you think that your growth is limited or that you cannot hone your potential? If you are truthful, you will admit that it happens when you fixate on the negatives.

And when do you focus on the negatives?

Like most people, you probably focus on negativities when you don't have the strength and positivity to look at what's good in your life.

And what does that boil down to? A lack of gratitude!

How the Absence of Gratitude Breeds Scarcity

The mere thought of not having enough leads to a series of similar thoughts that take your attention towards the negatives in life. The more you observe them, the stauncher your belief about your growth being fixed to a specific limit only become.

On the other hand, expressing your thankfulness for a bowl of soup makes you understand the plight of those who don't have a bite to eat. That one acknowledgment makes you notice another blessing.

For example, you may acknowledge your chipped dinner plate and feel thankful for it. From that, your attention moves to the old couch you are sitting on, and you feel happy about at least having some piece of furniture.

Gratitude causes a chain reaction: one thing leads to another. Within minutes, you realize that you may not have everything, but you have enough. This acknowledgment alleviates your whining.

When the complaining subsides, you find more space in your mind and life to think about what you wish to do, and that's how you start to hone your potential, realize your goal, and then pursue them to create abundance in your life.

It is as simple as that, and this simplicity can be your way of life.

With this connection now clearer to you, let's focus on the traits of those with a scarcity mindset and how to overcome those.

"In all affairs, it's a healthy thing now and then to hang a question mark on the things you have long taken for granted."

Bertrand Russell

Are You Enjoying
Empower Your Gratitude?

Now you can enjoy the audiobook while exercising, driving, gardening or relaxing in your favorite chair.

Chapter 8: Traits of A Scarcity Mindset and How to Improve Them

"Got no checkbooks, got no bank; still, I'd like to express my thanks. I got the sun in the morning and the moon at night."

Irving Berlin

Irving Berlin's quote is the mantra of those with a gratitude mindset. That's how they roll, and that's how they attract massive abundance their way.

Those with the scarcity mindset: not so much! And that is why their hearts and banks are never satisfied.

To be amongst the grateful ones, you have to get rid of the scarcity mindset. Understanding its traits can help you figure out whether this mindset has victimized you.

Let's focus on that:

7 Traits of Those with a Poverty Mindset

I won't just share the traits of the poverty mindset. I'll also compare it with the abundant mindset to give you a clearer picture of how both function, which will allow you to make the right choice.

1. **Think small:** Sadly, the poverty mindset restricts your ability to think. Your thoughts wander in a limited direction too, and you feel scared of dreaming big, mainly because you think you cannot achieve your dreams.

   On the contrary, the abundant mindset makes you courageous. You aren't afraid to dream big because you know seeing it is believing, and that once you put your heart and mind to it, you will make the unimaginable come to life.

2. **Focus on what's lacking:** The scarcity mindset narrows down your vision to the extent that you only notice what's lacking in your life. You can see how you don't have a job, or a loving partner, or cannot go on exotic holidays, but you are blind to all the other joys your life has to offer, such as the warmth of your friends, the ability to read and write, waking up to see the sun, etc.

    In contrast, the abundant mindset always focuses on seeing the bounties in the present moment. That's why it makes you believe that you have access to everything in plenty, which is why you successfully manifest what you want.

3. **Nurture resentments:** With the poverty mindset, you are always oblivious to the goodness in life, which is why you are mostly remorseful about the moments you have missed, the mistakes you made, the failures you had, and worry incessantly about how nothing will ever work out for you. That explains why you stay stagnant in life: because you focus on complaining instead of celebrating more.

    On the other hand, once you nurture the gratitude mindset, you become an optimist. You learn from experiences, focus on growth, make the most of every moment, and gradually climb up the 'happiness and success' ladder.

4. **Fear change:** Change is scary for everyone, but a scarcity mindset makes you resist it so much that even the thought of it causes shivers down your spine. You believe you can never survive change because you don't have the guts to embrace and endure it.

    Conversely, with an abundant mindset, you become open to the idea of accepting and exploring changes to see what it brings your way because you find something positive even in the darkest of times. That's how you power through and make it to the finish line.

5. **Makes you reactive:** Since negativity plagues you when you have a poverty mindset, you become reactive to every situation,

good or bad, in life. You may think reacting to a positive-seeming experience is beneficial, but that's why you end up making hasty decisions. However, without thinking things through, you make shots in life and often complain about how things went wrong.

Contrariwise, the abundant mindset turns you into a proactive individual. It turns you into someone who analyzes things, assesses the opportunity costs of different choices, weighs their pros and cons, and then makes a strategic choice and plan. By doing this, you end up making wise decisions that foster your happiness and well-being.

6. **You think you know it all:** Although the poverty mindset restricts your vision, you become conservative to the idea of growth because you believe you know it all and have achieved it all too.

   Since you struggle to look beyond the boundaries you have created, you don't realize the need to learn and grow. That explains why stagnancy dances in your life so much.

   Conversely, this changes for the better with an abundant mindset. The abundance mentality yearns for knowledge, wisdom, and growth. With that mindset, you have a never-ending thirst for skills, knowledge, and intellect, and you try to learn something new every day, which is why you keep achieving new feats.

7. **Allows your intense emotions to control you:** Human beings are emotional creatures, so it is fine to experience intense emotions. That said, it is unwise to hold onto them, allowing them to control and then sabotage you. That is what usually happens when you have a scarcity mindset.

   Fixating on the negatives in life makes you experience volatile emotions that you embrace and never let go of as you should. Your erratic emotions make you concentrate on all that does not work in your life, and you find your growth going down the drain.

Contrariwise, the abundant mindset helps you get out of this rut by allowing you to acknowledge your emotions without holding onto them in any way. You learn to handle them effectively, ensuring they don't cloud your judgment or compel you to make reactive decisions. As a result, you always think about what works for you, act calmly, and put your best foot down in life.

This comparison should have given you a good enough idea of where you stand concerning the poverty and abundant mindset. Now, here's what you need to do next.

How to Take a Step Forward to Overcome the Scarcity Mindset

As limiting as the scarcity mindset is, it is easy to overcome by swapping it with the abundant mindset. Here's how you can achieve this goal:

- Observe your thoughts, attitude, and behavior for a couple of days, keeping the traits of the scarcity mindset in consideration.

- Ensure that you pay attention to how you react when things don't pan out as you expected. Take note of how little or more you complain daily. Observe your attitude towards learning and trying new things.

- Keep jotting down points as you observe something in your personality.

- Even if you have a single trait of the scarcity mindset that you practice too often, you nurture a poverty mindset.

- Now your job is to take baby steps every day to rectify this. I'll share the guidelines in detail in the next chapter.

- For now, begin by chanting this suggestion day in and day out, *"I have an abundant life, and I am thankful for it."*

- As you chant this mantra, visualize yourself living a bountiful life full of moment-to-moment happiness. Think of whatever fortune you wish to have in life, and imagine experiencing it.

If you start doing that daily, you will be amazed at how positive you start feeling in a matter of days. To capitalize on this momentum, follow the steps highlighted in the next chapter.

"The world gives you way more than you ever give it."

Kamal Ravikant

Chapter 9: Replacing the Scarcity Mindset with the Abundant Mentality

"I would maintain that thanks are the highest form of thought and that gratitude is happiness doubled by wonder."

G. K. Chesterton

The more you explore gratitude, the more it flourishes, which is one of the things that makes it so unique: it *multiplies with each minute of practice and soon fills your heart and life with beauty, magic, and serenity.*

You want the same, don't you?

Then you have to get rid of the scarcity mindset for good?

Here's what you need to do.

#1: Think and dream big

Start small by just giving power to your dreams. Think of what you wish to achieve in life and do so without putting in the restriction of time, money, or other constraints.

If you wish to paraglide, think of paragliding in the most beautiful locations and even starting a paragliding school someday if that's what you want. If you want to be rich, don't just think of making a thousand dollars more than what you're currently making; dream of being a billionaire. It all starts with big dreams, and then the rest becomes history.

#2: Focus on the Plenty

Every time your mind focuses on what is lacking in your life, steer it towards what's in plenty. You may not realize it instantly, but things will become visible to you if you put a positive spin on everything.

Think of the many smiles you get from friends and family. Think of the abundance of rays of sunshine. Think of the countless minutes of happiness you get from playing with your child. Shift your focus towards what's abundant, and abundance shall patronize you too.

#3: Ditch the resentments

Instead of always fixating on what went wrong and the many failures you have had in life, think of what could go right if you start to think positively. If you focus on the one positive thing you can do right now, answers and solutions will start coming to you.

Also, ask yourself positive questions. Instead of asking, 'why did I fail?', ask yourself, 'how can I succeed this time around?' Your brain answers you according to the connotation of the questions you ask yourself. If you ask negative questions, negativity is what you get. Instead, start asking yourself positive questions, and remorsefulness will soon be a thing of the past.

#4: Embrace change

Change is a constant part of all our lives. No matter what happens in your life from one moment to the next, things will always change. The sooner we accept this, the easier it becomes to move on. Rather than resisting change, embrace it. "How can I do that," you may ask?

Well, whenever you encounter a change, take a few moments to calm yourself down. Take deep breaths, and then ask yourself if there is one good thing hidden in the change. The instant you build the keenness to see it, you will identify it and move forward positively.

#5: Become proactive

A proactive attitude leads to success. To develop such an attitude, improve your reactive behavior. Emotional intelligence plays a significant role in this area, and I'll throw light on that in one of the following sections.

For now, start to think things through before putting your foot down. If you are starting a business, understand its different aspects. If you are thinking of moving in with your partner, get to know him/her a bit more first.

Instead of jumping the gun, analyze a situation, detail out possible routes you could take, compare every choice, and then decide based on what feels right to you.

#6: Develop a thirst to learn

Those who learn always grow, and have many places to go, both literally and figuratively. You can enjoy the same by building the habit of learning more. Begin by just picking your current skill set or profession and looking for something new and easy to learn in that area.

Perhaps you could learn of short keys on MS Word or some formula in Excel. Maybe you could discover a new feature in your smartphone that you haven't explored before. Just keep learning, and you will be surprised at how your horizons broaden with time.

Make a habit of these practices by engaging in them regularly. Setting reminders on your phone is a good way to ensure that.

You also need to build your emotional awareness and intelligence in the process. Since this is quite a vast topic, let's discuss it in the following section on mindfulness.

"Feeling gratitude and not expressing it is like wrapping a present and not giving it."

William Arthur Ward

Gratitude unlocks the **fullness** of life. It turns what we have into enough, and more. It turns denial into **acceptance**, chaos to order, confusion to **clarity**. It can turn a meal into a feast, a house into a home, a stranger into a **friend**.

— *Melody Beattie*

Section 4

Gratitude and Mindfulness

"Piglet noticed that even though he had a Very Small Heart, it could hold a rather large amount of Gratitude.

A.A. Milne

Introduction to Section 4: Gratitude and Mindfulness

Winnie the Pooh is one of the most beloved stories and animated series. Besides kids, adults like it too because of the wonderful wisdom and love for life expressed beautifully in the book.

This quote mentioned at the start of this section is a reminder of what it takes to cultivate gratitude: an intention to be grateful. The size of the heart doesn't matter all that much. Once you are thankful, your gratitude ultimately makes your heart bigger, not in size, but warmth, love, and happiness.

Piglet successfully harbored and manifested gratitude because he was mindful of the power of gratitude, its effect on one's life, and his emotions. Mindfulness is a must-nurture state of mind that is rudimentary to empowering your gratitude.

You may have different ideas about mindfulness, which is perfectly fine because virtues, states, and feelings are subjective: they mean different things from one person to the next.

However, it is crucial to explore it in the context of gratitude so you understand the relationship between the two. This section focuses on this particular aspect only.

Chapter 10: The Relationship between Mindfulness and Gratitude

"It's a funny thing about life; once you begin to take note of the things you are grateful for, you begin to lose sight of the things that you lack."

Germany Kent

Gratitude cannot thrive in the absence of the right perspective that shifts your attention from what's lacking to what's enough. When that's the case, your perspective becomes positive, and when you perceive things positively, you start feeling content and delighted.

Your ability to perceive things positively and dwell in the present has a lot to do with your state of mindfulness.

Let start with a discussion of what mindfulness truly is, followed by its connection with gratitude.

Understanding Mindfulness

Mindfulness is the indescribable capacity to live in the present and experience the moment fully as it comes and embrace it without any ill-feeling, judgment, or bitterness.

Whether you are feeling angry at the moment, just dropped a glass that shatters to pieces, or taking a peaceful walk in the park, you focus only on the moment without worrying about anything else.

As we work on our tasks, we constantly think about the past or the future. The 'ifs' and the 'buts' never really leave us. Worries of the future and regrets of the past haunt us.

Moreover, we tend to analyze and experience things based on our preconceived notions. You may never try tomatoes your entire life or try to enjoy the fruit simply because you did not like it the only time you had it in your childhood. You may not see the wisdom locked in an acquaintance's words because you once had a heated argument with him.

Rehashing the past, fretting about the future uncertainties, and using your preconceived notions as a measure to analyze and judge experiences, people, ideas, and thoughts weigh you down. It also makes you remorseful, bitter, negative, and causes you to harbor a scarcity mindset. Called forgetfulness, this state of mind has a detrimental impact on your wellbeing.

Only by solving these issues can gratitude make its way into your heart and life. That is where mindfulness comes in handy:

How Mindfulness Fosters Gratitude and Vice Versa

Here's how mindfulness and gratitude complement each other and inject lots of laughter, excitement, and pleasure into your life:

- Often rarely acknowledge our blessings at the moment because our thoughts are lurking in the past or future. When we are mindful, we stay in the present, and when our present is the abode of our thoughts, our eyes and mind become receptive to our blessings around us, and we start acknowledging them.

- We hold on to our mistakes and nurture hatred for ourselves and those who wronged us because we live in the past. Taking trips down memory lane is fine as long as you don't make your past your permanent abode. When you are mindful, you realize the importance of living in the here and now. You make your peace with your past, choose to move on, and that's how you become focused on the moment and grateful for it.

- Fulfillment and joy in life come from many things. One of those things is exploring your deep needs and aspiration, thereby understanding yourself better so you can do what brings you joy and meaning. Sometimes, doing that is tricky because we keep holding on to our preconceived notions and judge, observe and listen to things with a judgmental attitude.

If you constantly think about how you must never swim because you will drown, you may not pursue the one thing you have the potential for and will also enjoy. Mindfulness improves this attitude for the better, allowing you to become more receptive to experiences and ideas and embrace them with open arms, explore them and see what suits you best.

As you try new things, set meaningful goals, and make exciting discoveries about yourself, your life automatically becomes more worthwhile.

- Moreover, the inability to embrace the present also comes from being too possessive about our emotions. We take our emotions so seriously to the extent that we hold on to them for years. An emotion meant to have a lifespan of about 12 minutes goes on to rule our lives for months, even years, because we refused to let it go.

That's why fears, stress, worries, anger issues, frustrations, envious feelings, and the likes keep us from being grateful and happy in the here and now. The right antidote to the problem is to cultivate the gratitude mentality, and once you do that, you accept, understand, and handle your emotions effectively.

Consequently, this ability improves your emotional intelligence, allowing you to foster love in relationships, tranquility in life, and gratitude in your mind.

With all these positive changes coming into your life, your life becomes a joy to live and a haven for sure.

Let us talk about how to manifest this state of mindfulness in your life in the following chapters.

"In ordinary life, we hardly realize that we receive a great deal more than we give, and that it is only with gratitude that life becomes rich."

Dietrich Bonhoeffer

Chapter 11: Mindfulness-Based Practices to Cultivate Gratitude through Emotional Awareness

"Do not lose yourself in the past. Do not lose yourself in the future. Do not get caught in your anger, worries, or fears. Come back to the present moment, and touch life deeply. This is mindfulness."

Thich Nhat Hanh

The moment right here is your life: embrace it, live it, enjoy it.

Let me walk you through some easy and highly effective mindfulness-based practices to cultivate gratitude and become more invested in yourself and your life.

Embrace Your Emotions

We have eight basic emotions:

1. Anger
2. joy
3. trust
4. fear
5. surprise
6. sadness
7. disgust
8. envy.

All the other emotions we experience, including frustration, acceptance, vigilance, grief, terror, admiration, rage, and so on, stem from these eight.

While we are emotional beings, we are also quite wise, or, at the very least, we can also be astute. That happens well only when we learn to put a leash on our emotions.

Emotions are here to guide us. They often stir up due to the different experiences we have in life. We need to understand them and treat them with kindness so that we don't hold onto them for any longer than we need to, and instead, use them to learn more about ourselves and how the environment shapes us—and how we shape it and influence others.

Here is how you can tame your emotions, understand them better, and use that awareness to cultivate the gratitude mentality.

- Every time you experience an intense emotion, whether that's fear, anger, envy, joy, or surprise, and you feel an urge to react to it, excuse yourself from the situation so you can sit peacefully with the emotion and explore it.

- If an emotion feels too powerful—for example, if either anger or fear feels powerful—take deep breaths to calm yourself down. Inhale through your nose to a count of 5 and exhale through your mouth to a count of 7. We inhale more when we feel anxious or stressed; hence, exhaling out more air naturally calms us down.

- As you feel calmer, try to name the exact emotion you feel. If you feel rage, what is the base emotion? When you identify it as anger, figure out whether there is an underlying emotion there. Often, anger comes from suppressed sadness, so spend some time understanding the exact emotion you are experiencing.

- Accept that emotion by chanting this affirmation, *"I am experiencing anger/joy/etc., and I embrace my emotion."* Once you accept your emotion as a part of you, any ill feeling you nurture for it starts to subside.

- The emotion will increase and plummet in intensity. Allow it to happen naturally; all the while, breathe deeply and softly chant the affirmation mentioned above.

- This practice also controls your urge to react to the emotion.

- In the end, think of what the emotion taught to you—or is trying to teach you and what triggered it. This awareness informs you about how you behave and how different situations affect you, allowing you to make better decisions.

- Be thankful to yourself and the emotion for this experience, and then move on.

Working on this practice every day makes you more receptive and gentler towards your emotions. As you understand them better with time, you find it easy to soothe jealousy, resentment, worry, and anger and become more grateful.

Shape Your Life According to What Your Emotions Teach You

If you allow wisdom to flow in you, you will realize how much you can learn from your emotions alone.

Often, life feels incomplete and meaningless because we don't make the right choices, which is often partly rooted in a lack of emotional awareness. You may feel unhappy with your career, which is why you are angry and ungrateful mostly.

What you don't realize is that your anger may be rooted in a lack of fulfillment that comes from not giving your job your best shot. If only you start to work hard enough, your productivity will rise, leading to better job satisfaction and ultimately gratitude.

As you start to accept and study your emotions, start using that knowledge to shape your life positively with gratitude.

- Figure out the different emotions you experience on meeting different people. If some folks make you feel negative, demotivated, and whiny, your emotions want you to avoid that so you can allow gratitude and positivity to enter your life.

- Pay attention to the different triggers that set off your volatile emotions. Perhaps long office hours drain you, and that's what makes you grumpy. If you shorten them and ease your workload, you may find it easier to relax and be grateful.

- Observe what your emotions say about your aspirations, talents, and genuine needs. Often, our needs are quite simple, and once we start to feel them, happiness and thankfulness automatically flow in your life.

As you get these insights about yourself, start to apply them in your life because that's how you use mindfulness to your advantage. To keep feeling more grateful, try the next set of gratitude strategies in the following chapter.

"We must find time to stop and thank the people who make a difference in our lives."

John F. Kennedy

Chapter 12: Be Mindful of the Blessings and Challenges in Life

"Strive to find things to be thankful for, and just look for the good in who you are."

Bethany Hamilton

There is plenty to be thankful for if you are mindful and have the intention to be grateful. To keep growing happier by the day, here are some of my most recommended practices:

Gratitude for Food

Food is quite an important part of our lives. We have around two to three meals daily, and many of us are gastronomes at heart, try new delicacies, and harbor great love for food. Unfortunately, not all of us express our gratitude for it daily or eat mindfully.

Many of us usually eat in a rush, gulping down one bite after another, eating bigger portion sizes, and having way too many helpings than we need to. We may enjoy those meals or feel we do, but we also forget about them too soon. Also, we often don't fully acknowledge what we eat, the textures and tastes of the food, and the value and the provided nutrition. Our goal is to eat more.

The right way to eat is to do so mindfully. You take small bites, chew them slowly and properly, notice the texture and taste of the bite, and then swallow it.

Mindful eating allows you to enjoy your food, eat only as much as you need to and relish what you consume, which ultimately makes you feel grateful for every bite you eat.

Doing that is important, and so, whether you have a biscuit or a full three-course meal, you feel grateful for it and surround yourself with an abundance of gratitude.

- Always start your meal with a prayer acknowledging the food on the table, whether it is just a toast or a breakfast of sausages, baked beans, toasts, and fruit. No matter how little or how much food you have, be thankful for it by saying something as simple as, *"I am thankful for the food I am eating and am blessed to have it."*

- Take a small bite and before you start chewing it, try to point out as many textures as you can feel and acknowledge each of them.

- Chew the bite slowly, about 30 times, if possible, before swallowing it.

- Try pinpointing the different tastes you feel. Instead of labeling something as 'bad' or 'not tasty,' figure out the exact taste. Is it bitter, too sour, burnt, bland? When you focus on pointing the exact taste instead of labeling the entire food item as good or bad, you treat it nonjudgmentally and accept it as it is.

- Once you have finished a serving, tune into your tummy to see if you <u>need</u> more food. If you feel satisfied, leave the table and end the meal on another note of gratitude.

- If you feel like having another helping, take a small one.

Start eating in this manner and draw a comparison between how grateful you feel about the food you eat and the entire act of eating with how you felt before you started eating this way. The results themselves will motivate you to stick to this practice.

Gratitude and Mindfulness for Your Life

Taking things for granted is something many of us are often guilty of. I am not saying you need to make a fuss about getting up to see a new morning every day. However, being grateful for your life is important because you never know when you may take your last breath.

Be grateful for your life because this is your reality.

- Upon waking up every morning, be thankful for opening your eyes and getting to see a new day.

- Pay your gratitude by chanting a positive affirmation such as, *"I am thankful for this day, and I will make the most of it."*

- Take a few moments to scan your body, from your toes to your head. Wriggle your toes, stretch your arms, snap your fingers, touch your head, and while doing so, be thankful for each of those body parts and the ability to move them.

- Take a few deep breaths and end the practice on a final note of gratitude and anticipation for the day.

Gratitude for Your Health

Similar to being grateful for your life, it is equally important to be thankful for your health. Never forget the old age adage, *'health is wealth.'*

- After paying gratitude for your life, you can carry a round of gratitude for your health. You can also carry out this practice at any other time of the day.

- Look at yourself in-depth and be thankful for being healthy. If you can breathe, move around, open and shut your eyes, walk and run, and carry out your routine chores comfortably, you are healthy and should be happy about it.

- If you have an ailment or two, be thankful for surviving irrespective of it and living your life. Whether you have diabetes, have high blood pressure, or contracted COVID-19, as long as you are breathing, be thankful for your health.

Here is a short list of good health-based affirmations you can chant:

- *"I am thankful for my health."*

- *"I feel healthy and happy."*

- *"With every breath that I take, I feel healthier than ever."*

- *"My body functions optimally, and I am grateful for it."*

- *"I am at my ideal body weight and feel good about myself."*

In the same way, nurture gratitude for your body and appearance.

Gratitude for Body and Appearance

Body shaming and many inner insecurities often cause us to harbor some ill feelings towards our bodies. Perhaps you aren't too fond of your double chin, wish your bingo wings could disappear, or feel bad about being short. Such resentments make us conscious of our body image and also make us take it for granted.

To create a harmonious life for yourself, you need to be grateful for every aspect of your existence and being. Your body is a part of your existence, and until you are thankful for it, your mind, heart, soul, and body won't feel in unison.

Here's a quick practice to nurture body positivity and be grateful for how you are and how you look.

- Lie flat on your back or keep sitting if that feels comfortable.

- Take a few deep breaths and start scanning your toes.

- As you wriggle and observe them, say a note of gratitude for having toes. 'Today, I am thankful for my toes.'

- Move a little further and pay gratitude for your feet.

- Keep moving similarly towards your head and express your gratefulness for every part of your body that you encounter in that process.

- While doing so, pay attention to how you feel about every body part, and see if any negative feelings get stirred up. For instance, if you don't like your flabby arms, think of why you feel that way. Acknowledge that feeling and question its authenticity. As you explore the reasons, remind yourself of how you must accept and love yourself regardless of how others feel about you. Practice self-acceptance affirmations such as:

- *"I accept and love my body as it is."*

- *"My body is beautiful, and I love it."*

- *"At this moment, I choose to accept myself fully."*

- *"My body is a reservoir of positivity."*

- *"I am thankful for my healthy body."*

Start using these affirmations regularly to build a lifelong habit of being grateful for the person you are. It will take you a couple of weeks to achieve it, yes, but you will feel grateful in every moment and every aspect once you do.

Let us now move forward and look at another aspect of gratitude: gratitude and its related challenges.

"May the work of your hands be a sign of gratitude and reverence to the human condition."

Mahatma Gandhi

I don't have to chase **extraordinary** moments to find happiness - it's right in front of me if I'm paying attention and **practicing gratitude**.

— *Brene Brown*

Section 5

Gratitude and Challenges

"Enjoy the little things, for one day you may look back and realize they were the big things."

Robert Brault

Introduction to Section 5: Gratitude and Challenges

Challenges are a part of everyone's journey, no matter how big or small it is, or easy or difficult it seems.

Similarly, some challenges are bound to come your way when you start to empower your gratitude. I know it seems like an oddity. After all, if gratitude makes your life tranquil, then why would this journey be laced with obstacles, right?

As beautiful as gratitude is, and irrespective of the huge amount of peace it brings in your life, like everyone in this world, you will confront some challenges because of the following reasons:

- If you are new to gratitude, you have probably had a complaining attitude and a scarcity mindset for quite a while now. As determined as you are to break it, it will not be a straightforward journey. There will be times when you resort to whining, which will be a considerable challenge in itself.

- Even if you have been grateful from time to time, expressing your thankfulness for every moment and everything you do can become overwhelming at first because you feel like doing the same thing again. This task at times feels like clockwork, and if you have a habit of negative self-talk, you may weigh yourself down.

- Looking at the positives in life is great, but it gets tougher amidst challenges. If you are experiencing one failure after another, you may find it quite hard to say thanks for surviving it.

- Another challenge surrounding gratitude is hyper-focus, a state of such deep concentration that you forget everything around yourself and become fully engrossed in a certain task.

  As soothing and as beneficial as this state sounds, this state can at times divert your attention from other important tasks and keep you engrossed in something that may not be meaningful for a long while. While being grateful, it is also important to move on in life and carry on with routine chores, and for that, you must manage your state of hyper-focus.

There is an effective solution for all these challenges, and the chapters in this section will discuss them one by one.

Chapter 13: Gratitude for Failures and Obstacles

"Cultivate the habit of being grateful for every good thing that comes to you and to give thanks continuously. And because all things have contributed to your advancement, you should include all things in your gratitude."

Ralph Waldo Emerson

Gratitude for Rejection

Rejection tends to be quite hard-hitting, especially when it comes on unexpectedly. If someone denies you something you have been hoping for, or have desired for a long time, naturally, it hits you hard and is difficult to digest right away.

Whether it's a job application panel rejecting you or someone you have had a crush on for years failing to reciprocate the same feelings, rejection in any form can be difficult to fathom and bear.

Naturally, when you feel denunciated, you feel frustrated and angry, making it tricky to be grateful in the present. However, in times like these, you need to uphold your gratitude the most to persevere and move forward towards better days.

- First, acknowledge the rejection you have experienced and write it down in clear words.

- It is important to validate your feelings and to embrace your agony. At times, we try to shove our pain down in hopes of feeling better. We become dispassionate to it, don't talk about it, and keep ignoring it. That only does you more harm than good because pain tends to intensify when it goes unacknowledged. Hence, always acknowledge your hurt first and detail out how it makes you feel.

- Now, very gently think of any hidden positives in the situation. Perhaps it has made you realize any of your weaknesses that you can now improve on to avail a better opportunity. For example, if you were rejected for a job, maybe build a skill to apply for an even higher paying job next.

- Also, think of how the dismissal shapes you into a stronger version of yourself, one who does not give up and keeps moving on.

- Moreover, use it as an opportunity to get clarity about what you want. Perhaps you did not genuinely love the girlfriend who refused your marriage proposal; perhaps you only believed it to be love guided by your superficial desires.

- Also, think of how even better things await you at the end of the road. You will experience them if you keep going.

- As you note down all these positives, express your gratitude for each of them slowly and consciously. For example, while uttering the words, *"I am thankful for this experience,"* do so slowly so that the vibration of every word rings in your ear, making you more conscious of them.

It takes a lot of courage to be grateful in times of rejection, but you can do it; all you have to do is tap into the warrior power within you.

Gratitude for Failures

When you encounter a setback and things don't pan out as expected, it is normal to feel a little disheartened. This feeling is natural, and you must not shun it.

Nonetheless, it is important to be grateful, especially at such times, so you handle the failure openly and work towards improvements instead of sitting back in dismay.

When a mishap hits you, whether that's:

- Getting fired from your job

- Not winning an entrepreneurship challenge you were sure you'd win and get start-up capital for your business,

- Not getting into your desired business school or any other setback, acknowledge that you are going through a hard time.

- Writing or speaking about the experience helps to put your feelings out in the open instead of allowing them to rattle in your head.

- Work on calming your emotions as we focused on earlier, and once they soothe, think of what the experience taught you.

- Point out any three things from the setback. Even if you can only find one positive, push yourself to come up with at least three. Those could be anything such as getting a chance to polish your skills, improving your speaking skills, getting more time with your family, etc.

- Go through the list and express your gratitude for the seemingly unfortunate situation. You could say anything such as, *"I experienced this (name of setback) and have figured out the following positives from it for which I am extremely thankful."*

Doing this at first may seem hard, but soon, you will find in you the courage to be grateful even when you deem it unnecessary, and then you will build a habit of it, which will continue to add joy to your life.

"I would maintain that thanks are the highest form of thought, and that gratitude is happiness doubled by wonder."

Gilbert K. Chesterton

Chapter 14: How to Use Gratitude to Manage Greed

*"It is not joy that makes us grateful.
It is gratitude that makes us joyful."*

David Steindl-Rast

Gratitude is a lot like a magical elixir. As you know, sipping a magical elixir can make you immortal, youthful, wealthy, or anything that the elixir has powers for. Likewise, gratitude can bring forth many brilliant effects in your life.

No, gratitude cannot give you your youth back, change your mortality rate, or make you king of the world. All it can do—and do well at that—is equip you with the capacity to manage many of life's problems that would have otherwise seemed daunting and impossible to take on and triumph over.

Here are some more issues that you may confront as you walk the path towards a more grateful life, along with guidelines on how to overcome them.

Gratitude and Greed

It's human nature to want more, which is why many of us want the 'best of everything.' Unfortunately, that means we often forget that "the best" is a subjective term, and so, naturally, its meaning varies from person to person.

Once you start pursuing it, there may never be an end to it. That's because when you achieve a certain mark, you realize you can have more. For example, after buying a three-bedroomed house, you then yearn for one with six rooms and a huge backyard. On buying the latest model of Mercedes, you start aspiring for another luxury car.

Some of us tend to find loopholes around this aspect, stating that the desire to have more keeps us moving forward and motivates us to accomplish bigger and better goals. However, the reality is that there exists a stark distinction between achieving bigger goals and being greedy.

We can describe greed as a selfish and intense desire for food, power, wealth, love, abundance, and other similar things. When you become greedy, you never feel content.

On the other hand, the pursuit of challenging goals and the journey to improve yourself feels different. You try to shape yourself into a better individual and set meaningful goals while feeling content with the outcomes, even the unexpected ones. Your gratitude for what you have separates the two.

- To keep greed at bay, ensure to take stock of your blessings every day.

- Whenever you experience an intense desire to have something, always take a moment to reflect on the desire. Next, assess its authenticity, importance, and nature.

- Ask yourself questions like, *"Is it something I truly want? "What emotions does it stem from?" "What value does it have in my life?"* ETC.

- Reflect on the answers, write them down and be grateful for that awareness.

Greed tends to be overpowering, but don't forget that you are a more powerful being. Use your abilities well, and no amount of greed can ever dampen your spirits.

Let us move to the following chapter and discuss how gratitude can help with two more challenges: hyper-focus and the monkey state of mind.

"Gratitude is not only the greatest of virtues but the parent of all others."

Marcus Tellius Cicero

Chapter 15: Gratitude and Focus Issues

"Gratitude paints little smiley faces on everything it touches."

Richelle E. Goodrich

With gratitude, even the sappy things become happier, and life becomes all the more blissful. That said, two more challenges associated with it have to do with focus.

Your focus needs to be straight and on the present moment; that way, you can manifest gratefulness in your life. Unfortunately, being in such a state tends to be a problem at times, especially since many of us have a habit of multitasking and thinking of many things simultaneously.

Here are two focus-related issues related to gratitude and, how you can use gratitude to overcome them.

Gratitude and Monkey State of Mind

The name "monkey state of mind" is a pantomime of how monkeys behave in jungles: leaping from one branch to another, always in a constant state of motion. Likewise, the human mind behaves similarly: jumping from one branch of thought to another, constantly thinking about one thing or another.

While we leap from one thought to another, we are also rushing to and from many tasks. You may be sending emails, cooking spaghetti, doing laundry, and also helping your kid do his math homework at the same time.

You may have built a habit of thinking and working this way, but this isn't healthy. First, it keeps you from being grateful in the moment because your attention is torn between too many things at once, which can feel overwhelming and stressful.

In addition, this habit of wandering off in thought also hinders your progress towards gratitude. You find yourself constantly in between thoughts of the past and future, which keeps you from anchoring yourself to the present moment. For you to be grateful, dwelling in the present moment is mandatory because that's how you take stock of your blessings.

Here is how you can fix this upsetting problem:

- Slowly, build the habit of doing one task at a time. If you are preparing a meal, do that first and then wash the dishes. If you are doing the dishes, control the urge to move back and forth to the lounge to check your email.

- Keep track of your thoughts. When thinking of an idea, please write it down to ensure you work on it solely.

- If your drift off in thought, acknowledge that unnecessary thinking has occurred.

- Take a few deep breaths to bring your attention back to the present moment, and then continue working on the task.

- Continue affirming gratitude-based suggestions to yourself, such as, *"I am working on this (name of task) and feel happy about it,"* or *"I am happy to be in this moment and grateful for it."*

It will take you some time, but if you are consistent with the practice, you will break your monkey state of mind and build a mindful one.

Gratitude and Hyper Focus

As described in an earlier chapter of this section, hyper-focus happens when you become engrossed in a task or thought to the extent that you struggle to leave it and engage in anything else. It is certainly good to become fully invested in a task but, being productive in different areas can be tricky if that's the only thing you do.

When it comes to gratitude, sometimes you may find that you become so overwhelmed with being grateful that you don't push yourself to do anything else at all. For example, you may become so content with living from paycheck to paycheck that you may not realize your genuine aspiration to be self-employed or start your organic farming project. Such a thing can keep you from living a meaningful and empowered life.

Here's a list of how gratitude can help you manage a state of hyper-focus:

1. Set a time frame for all your important tasks. For instance, if you have to write a blog post, dedicate an hour to it from 4 pm to 5 pm.

2. When it is time to work on something, begin it with gratitude and carry out the steps mindfully.

3. Set a timer to ensure you don't lose track of time.

4. When the timer beeps, consciously and a bit forcefully, stop engaging in the task. If you are writing and the timer buzzes off, stop writing right away.

5. Go through your progress in a few minutes and be thankful for it.

6. Even if you haven't accomplished much, be thankful for it and then move to another task.

7. Also, keep revisiting the genuine aspirations that you jotted down earlier and make time to pursue them.

With practice and consistency, you can easily work on this issue and become more focused, productive, and empowered than before.

I have shared many gratitude techniques in the chapters so far. Now I'd like to discuss the practice of gratitude separately to ensure you become aware of more beneficial techniques living a life of gratitude has to offer.

"Let us rise up and be thankful, for if we didn't learn a lot today, at least we learned a little, and if we didn't learn a little, at least we didn't get sick, and if we got sick, at least we didn't die; so, let us all be thankful." — **Buddha**

Happiness cannot be traveled to, owned, earned, worn or consumed. Happiness is the **spiritual experience** of living every minute with love, grace, and **gratitude**.

— *Denis Waitley*

Section 6

Gratitude and Practice

"There are only two ways to live your life. One is as though nothing is a miracle. The other is as though everything is a miracle."

Albert Einstein

Introduction to Section 6: Gratitude and Practice

With a grateful heart and mind, you see miracles everywhere because you realize how life in itself is a joy you must celebrate every day.

When it comes to practicing gratitude, it is important to nurture a habit of doing so. Just like you cannot expect to become muscular after a day's work-out, it is illogical to expect bounties to flow towards you and for your heart to become warm and loving after a few minutes of expressing your gratitude to the universe and the world around you. You have to work on it every single day, several times a day.

Also, while doing that, it is wise to be creative with practicing gratitude. Similar to how you find your life becoming mundane if you just have one activity to carry out, you may find yourself losing interest in exercising gratitude if you practice it using one technique only.

The beautiful thing about gratitude is that you can practice it in many different ways, and there is no hard and fast rule to doing so.

The chapters within this section will share plenty of ways to cultivate **gratefulness every day of your life**.

Chapter 16: Daily Gratitude Practices

"Some people grumble that roses have thorns;
I am grateful that thorns have roses."

Alphonse Karr

As I mentioned earlier, the key to nurturing gratitude is shifting your perspective.

Instead of whining about how you find thorns on a rose stem, why not be thankful for the thorns that seem accompanied by a beautiful bloom? The 'perspective shift' tends to be slightly difficult, especially in the beginning, considering how conditioned we are to complain more about our daily routines.

Fortunately, all that this is about to change. You have already ignited that spark by reading this book and working on the strategies discussed so far; all you need to do is level things up a notch.

If you are reading this book from this spot, this is a great place to start since it reveals some of the most powerful practices you can do daily to exercise gratitude.

Create a Morning Gratitude List

Make a habit of jotting down five things you are grateful for in the morning. From waking up in a cozy room, looking forward to a productive day, going back to the office after months of COVID-19 lockdown, to sipping coffee, note down any five things every morning you feel happy about, and express your gratitude for them.

It is a good idea to dedicate a separate journal or a section of your journal to your 'morning gratitude list.' You can go through the entire list in the morning, especially if you feel cranky and don't know what to be thankful for at that moment.

Curate Your Evening Gratitude List

This list is similar to the morning list.

The primary difference is that you will craft this list in the evening. As you snuggle under the covers at the end of each day, play the entire day's whereabouts in your head and note down any five things you feel grateful for.

From closing a deal, having a good chat with an old friend, seeing your kid have a good time at school, to having a nice dinner with your partner, recall all those happy moments of the day, and write them down.

In a few nights, you'll build a habit of this practice and inadvertently recall the good parts of the day to brighten up your mood instantly.

Keep a Gratitude Journal of Positive Affirmations

Take a notebook, and jot down different gratitude-based positive affirmations in it.

Sometimes, the routine life troubles and unexpected obstacles take such a toll on our mental well-being that it becomes difficult to exercise gratitude. This journal comes in very handy in such times; it gives you ideas of what to be grateful for and how.

- *"I am thankful for this new day."*

- *"I am grateful for the person I am and the life I have."*

- *"I am happy and grateful for this new season."*

- *"I am happy and spread happiness around."*

- *"I feel content in this moment of my life."*

- *"From food to clothes to shelter to relationships, I have everything I need, and I am grateful for that."*

- *"I am grateful for being alive."*

- *"I am thankful for being able to move around."*

- *"I am grateful for the senses I have."*

- *"I am grateful for having the ability to be thankful for my blessings."*

You can keep adding more affirmations to the list. Then, now and then, go through them to recall your blessings and feel inspired to be more grateful.

Try Different Ways to Say Thank You

You can also try different ways to say thank you. Saying thank you is a gesture of being grateful to someone, and there are so many ways to be creative with it.

Here's a list of ideas to get you moving forward:

- *"Thank you so much for your help!"*

- *"I am so grateful to you."*

- *"You are such a kind soul."*

- *"This is so wonderful of you."*

- *"Thanks a million!"*

- *"You just made my day."*

- *"Thank you for cheering me up."*

- *"Your positivity and compassion inspire me."*

- *"How thoughtful of you to do this."*

- *"I could not have pulled it off without your help."*

- *"I appreciate all your kindness and help."*

- *"Thank you for being in my corner."*

- *"Thank you for your support and guidance."*

- *"I owe you one, big time!"*

- *"Thank you for responding so fast."*

- *"Thank you for being around."*

These are all the different ways you can express your gratefulness, admiration, and love for different people. Use these to thank people according to the nature of the situation, type of person, and your relationship.

Let us now move to the following chapter and share some meditation-based techniques to manifest thankfulness.

"The deepest craving of human nature is the need to be appreciated."

William James

Chapter 17: Gratitude and Meditation

"Meditation is being in tune with our inner universe."

Anonymous

Meditation means many different things to different people. Some describe it as a state of mind, some define it as a tool to nurture mindfulness, and some refer to it as just being one with the moment.

No matter how you choose to describe meditation, its essence lies in accepting the moment and focusing every ounce of your attention on it, so in that very moment, you become united with the here and now and experience it fully.

Meditation is about instilling in yourself the awareness to focus on the moment alone and whatever it entails. By instilling this state in yourself, you become mindful and grateful.

Here are meditation-based practices to take your gratitude to the next level:

Gratitude Based Meditative Technique

Simply observing anything in the present, looking at the ceiling and thinking about nothing else, and concentrating on any one word at a time is meditation in its simplest manner.

That stated, here is a quick and easy gratitude meditation that works well for novices.

- Set a timer for 2 minutes if 10 minutes seems a lot for you in the beginning. However, if you can meditate for 10 minutes, that's great! Build up to it in the next few days and weeks to come.

- Find a quiet place where you can meditate for a little while without being interrupted.

- It is best to focus on this practice alone and not carry it out while driving, doing laundry, or carrying out any other chore.

- Sit straight in a stable, comfortable position keeping your head, back, and neck straight.

- You can even lie down if that feels easier.

- Close your eyes, or maintain gentle focus on any point about six to twelve feet in front of you.

- Take a relaxed breath, inhaling deeply from your nose, and exhaling through your mouth.

- Pay attention to the breath for a few moments. Pay close attention to how the air moves inside, around, and outside of your body.

- Scan your body for any part or area where you feel soreness, tension, warmth, or any tightness—we discussed this in the body scan meditation practice.

- As you draw in your next inhalation, imagine peace flowing in that area, replacing all the pain with love and warmth.

- To align yourself better with this moment, think of any other thoughts, plans, memories, or anything else that may constantly appear in your awareness. Then, inhale and think of those things, then allow those thoughts to flow out of your system as you breathe out.

- In a minute, you will feel your emotions, thoughts, and body become clearer and more spacious than before. This will make it easier to focus on the things you wish to extend your gratitude for.

- Very gently, think of how you have the biggest gift in the universe: the gift of life. Reflect on the fact that your mother gave birth to you, someone took care of feeding you milk, someone changed your diapers, someone bathed and clothed you, and as you grew older, someone was in charge of raising you.

The person you have become has resulted from a lot of time, attention, and energy, and you need to be thankful for that.

- Next, be thankful for having the gift of hearing. It is an incredibly important gift, one that we sometimes take for granted. Think of how this sense helps you hear things around you and even learn from them.

Think about how rewarding it is to listen to the chirping of a bird, the reporting of a newscaster, the melody played by an orchestra, your voice, and that of all your loved ones.

- Think of the gift of having a steady heartbeat, pumping fresh blood to your organs, keeping you alive. This gift makes you alive; use this moment to think of how valuable it is.

- Now, take another moment to recall all the things in your life that add convenience, value, and comfort to it. With a flip of a switch, light shines in your room.

Just by turning the tap, you get drinkable water. With a simple thermostat, you can adjust a room's temperature and make it cooler or warmer as per your needs. By pressing a few buttons on your phone, you can connect with loved ones. A few clicks, and you can access any information you need online. The roof over your head keeps you dry during storms and blocks out the scorching heat in the summers.

Everywhere you look around you, there is something to keep you safe, something to make your life more comfortable, and something to improve your efficiency and productivity. Think of all these things and be grateful for them.

It takes consistency to build a habit. Keep setting reminders and focus on the benefits of meditation to turn it into a habit because that's how you will cultivate the ability to be grateful in every moment.

Let's take this journey further and share some more gratitude practices in the next chapter.

"Entitlement is such a cancer, because it is void of gratitude."

Adam Smit

Chapter 18: Gratitude Practices to Infuse Joy in Every Moment

"Thank you is the best prayer that anyone could say; I say that one a lot. Thank you expresses extreme gratitude, humility, understanding."

Alice Walker

The best thing is, there exist many ways to offer this prayer of 'gratitude.' Here are some quick practices to make every moment of your life more delightful and meaningful.

Practice Self-Compassion

Being kind and loving to yourself is one of the secrets to a happy, well-balanced life. But, unfortunately, it is one thing many of us ignore.

Self-compassion does more than make you feel good about yourself; it's also a means of thanking yourself for going through the daily grind of life, striving for happiness in the face of adversity, and cultivating gratitude every day. It acknowledges your efforts and motivates you to keep powering on.

Say kind words to yourself and try to talk positively to yourself at all times. Every time you hear words or phrases in your head that suggest you are not good enough or that you are a failure, replace them with positive suggestions such as the following:

- *"I am kind and loving."*

- *"I love myself."*

- *"I am doing well in life."*

- *"I feel happy and positive."*

- *"I am surviving and growing better with each passing day."*

- *"Love surrounds me."*

- *"I am confident and strong."*

- *"I am a compassionate soul."*

- *"I have many talents that I utilize efficiently."*

Put these three steps into action:

1. Do your best to try to figure out your genuine needs and find ways to fulfill them.
2. Treat yourself to something nice and rewarding now and then to encourage yourself to keep up with all the good work you have been doing in life.
3. Forgive yourself for your mistakes and avoid holding grudges against yourself. Instead, live in the present and make it worthwhile.

10 Minutes of Gratitude

Set your alarm for a quick 10-minute gratitude break twice a day. You could take it during your lunch break, after work, in between difficult tasks, or once you are back home and wish to unwind.

In those 10 minutes, think of the different things, experiences, people, thoughts, and anything else you feel grateful for. For example, you could be grateful for your daily experiences or something that didn't happen during the day.

Feel grateful for how your co-worker brought coffee for you, how your boss appreciated you, the sweet text you received from an old friend, and the thought of having a safe home to return to after work.

For 10 minutes, think of nothing else but your blessings, and you will be amazed at how quickly you feel calm and peaceful.

Be Grateful for Your Work

It is understandable how work seems to be hard, exhausting, and even suffocating at times, especially if you are in a job or line of work that you don't enjoy all that much.

Nonetheless, since your career is an important aspect of your life, it is important to nurture gratitude for it to ensure the thought of it does not make you cranky, allowing you to work peacefully and also enjoy your work.

- Every day before you start your work, think of any three positives about it. For example, you could think of how it helps you pay the bill, how it challenges you to do better, and how it helps you survive in life.

- Write down those positives and reflect on them.

- Next, think of jobless people and those who lost work due to the COVID-19 pandemic and be thankful for having the means to manage your expenses.

- Next, please take a moment to close your eyes and imagine yourself doing well at your job, particularly visualizing the one task you dread the most, and excelling at it.

- Carry on with this practice for 5 minutes, and then exercise it again during mid-day.

Soon enough, you will find yourself feeling better about your job and even enjoying it irrespective of the hardships that come along.

Keep a Journal of Gratitude Posts

You can take the gratitude quotes from this book, find some more online and create your very own notebook of gratitude quotes.

Then, whenever you feel dismayed, or demotivated, open up a leaf of the journal, glance at a gratitude quote, or read it out loud to allow love to flow inside of you. Within minutes, you will feel spiritually revived and ready to tackle the problem.

Send Gratitude Letters and Messages to People

Every day you can send a gratitude-filled text message, email, or even a picture of yourself with a gratitude note to at least one of your loved ones. You could even set days to be thankful to different family members, friends, relatives, and even colleagues. Once in a while, write a detailed gratitude letter to someone you love.

Covertly Do Something Nice for Someone

Expressing your gratitude does not have to be through the direct medium of saying a "thank you" every time. Doing something nice, that too for others without letting them know about it, is a great way to express your gratefulness to them and the universe.

Now and then, think of a loved one or anyone you know: your neighbor, co-worker, boss, or anybody else you think needs some love, compassion, and positivity, and do something nice for him/her. For example, you could send muffins to your sister at work without telling her, feed the neighbor's dog when he is in the backyard, send an anonymous parcel to your partner, or do anything else that can cheer up the person in question.

Moreover, look for strangers outside in need of any help. Perhaps you see an elderly lady doing groceries looking for some tomato soup, and you place some cans on an aisle next to her when she has her back against you.

When you know your anonymous acts are helping people smile, you will feel great about yourself.

Additionally, add some journaling and visualization-based gratitude strategies to your life because they reinforce your good habits. Let us discuss them in the following chapter.

"If you are really thankful, what do you do? You share."

W. Clement Stone

Chapter 19: Gratitude through Journaling and Visualization Techniques

"A grateful heart is a magnet for miracles."

Anonymous

A heart brimming with gratitude attracts more bountifulness because it has learned and mastered the art of seeing the good in everything. Nothing ever appears bad or impossible because there is some good, some possibility locked in it always, and that's how that heart makes you grow more prosperous in life.

Here are some journaling and visualization-based techniques to ensure gratitude finds its way into your heart.

Practice Gratitude Visualization

Visualization practices use imagery to help you create scenarios in your head, believe in them, and attract those or similar experiences towards you. The human mind cannot distinguish between reality and imagination. It accepts whatever you believe.

This is where gratitude-based visualization comes into play. It is an easy and effective way to integrate gratitude in your mind, so it becomes a constant in your life.

Here is how you can practice:

1. Carve out 10 minutes of your routine and use this time to sit somewhere nice and quiet.

2. Sit comfortably and close your eyes.

3. Imagine a glowing light entering your heart and peacefully spreading to every nook of your body.

4. As it grows stronger, imagine that you feel lighter, happier, and more optimistic than before.

5. The light now emanates from you spread out.

6. That light is gratitude, and as it has filled your heart and body, you are now in a place to spread joy around.

7. In addition, picture yourself enjoying the routine pleasures of life and the many gifts your life has to offer you.

As you work on this practice every day, you slowly start to believe that gratitude is a permanent part of your life, and find it easier to offer it.

Journal about Gratitude for 10 Minutes

When you enjoy thinking about your blessings, and visualizing yourself being grateful, journal about all the things you are thankful for and how being grateful adds value to your life.

For example, if you often found yourself being grumpy or only focused on the negatives in life, write about how gratitude has made you calmer, pleasant, and optimistic.

Go through these accounts daily; it reinforces your beliefs and helps you keep the bigger picture in sight: the need to be grateful at all times.

Recall your Joyful Moments

Make it a must to recall at least one happy moment in your life daily, be it alone or with a loved one(s.)

Think about the first time you rode a bike with your dad; or a family picnic to the beach with all your cousins; or the time you made a treehouse with your parents and spent the night in it with your best friend; or your first kiss with your partner whom you love very much.

Recalling happy moments adds joy to your life and makes you realize that you have many things for which to be thankful. Ensure that you keep adding more memories to these accounts and go through all of them at least once a month.

Write about Some Miracles in Life

There are some instances in life, especially the positive, happy ones, that you never thought would happen. Perhaps you had a huge win you thought you did not deserve, a job promotion you did not see coming your way or being nominated for a writer's award you thought was too grand for you.

All such times are the 'miracles' in your life; they give you more reasons to be grateful. Occasionally recall such experiences and write about how you never expected them to happen and how encountering them changed your life for the better.

If you received a scholarship to a great law school that opened up fantastic career opportunities for you, write about that and the fact that you were the 5 out of 1,500 applicants who received the scholarship.

You may think there is not much to be thankful for in life and that there are not many miracles, but if you adopt the right attitude, you will find something great in your life for sure, a miracle.

The more you work on these practices, the fonder you grow of them. That's when you take on to those practices like your second skin.

Kindness is a very important aspect of gratitude, and it plays a vital role in its practice. Let's focus on that next.

"If you count all your assets, you always show a profit."

Robert Quillen

Chapter 20: Gratitude and Kindness

"When you practice gratefulness, there is a sense of respect towards others."

Dalai Lama

This sense of respect is what you need to extend towards others to create social harmony and foster living with each other respectfully. Kindness is integral to building a healthy life for yourself and others. In this chapter, we discuss that aspect in detail.

Kindness is about being compassionate to yourself and others. Gratitude is about being thankful for what you have. And so, in a way, when you show compassion to others, you show them you care, which is a means to express your gratitude to them.

Although it may seem as if kindness is slipping away from this world, the truth is that it still exists in all of us. It only requires you to nurture a little care, affection, and the urge to be kind and supportive to one another. Once you start doing that, you automatically express your gratitude to other people and the universe.

Let us focus on some practical ways to practice kindness and gratitude.

Be Kind to Unkind People

I know this is a toughie and arguably the one thing you wouldn't want to do. That said, to wipe off hatred and toxicity from the world, we need more compassionate souls. For that to happen, you have to play your part.

It is one thing to draw your boundaries and not allow people to misuse you, but another thing to be kind to those who seem unkind. People often put up a tough exterior to shield themselves from the hurt and pain in the world. Melting that exterior requires a kind heart.

If you see a friend becoming withdrawn, a neighbor often scowling at you, and a co-worker being grumpy, go ahead and do something nice for them. For example, surprise them with chocolates, leave them sweet notes, or bring them warm food. Your kindness will soon make way to their heart, inspiring them to be kind too.

Nurture Empathy

Being compassionate is awesome; however, to connect with people and truly understand them, you need to nurture empathy. Empathy goes a step further than compassion and sympathy; it revolves around seeing and feeling yourself in someone else's shoes to experience their pain as yours.

Once you can genuinely feel the agony of another individual, you truly comprehend their pain and suffering. That's when you try to do something meaningful to help them out. Plus, you also become more aware of your blessings, which ultimately encourages you to be grateful for the many blessings in your life.

To be empathetic, focus more on the problems and pains of others. You don't need to poke around their issues; just imagine yourself in the rut they are stuck in and visualize yourself going through those tribulations. This scenario alone is enough to help you understand their misery and what you can do to help.

Moreover, instead of doubting their problems, labeling them as weak, or thinking of how tough life must be for them, be grateful for your life. Ups and downs are a part of everyone's life, but things become easier to bear when gratitude becomes part of the equation.

Perform One Act of Kindness Every Day

Make a list of different acts of kindness and ensure to do at least one every day. Here are some ideas for you:

- Make a bird feeder for the birds that frequent your backyard.

- Help any stray animal on the road.

- Help an older person cross the road.

- Call your parents and tell them how much you love them.

- Ask your co-worker if he/she needs assistance with work tasks.

- When you make coffee for yourself, ask others in the house if they need a cup too.

- Give your partner a nice massage.

- Be patient when you see the elderly climbing up and down the stairs and go slow.

- Get up and give your seat to the elderly, kids, expecting women, and anyone else on the bus or subway.

- If you see someone struggle to pay for a train ticket, offer to help—if you can.

- Participate in a shelter home, orphanage, or nursing home, and spread some smiles.

- Donate your clothes, books, shoes, utensils, and other items to good causes.

- Donate $50-$100 every month to a charitable organization working on a cause that resonates with your values.

- Be gentle with your subordinates when they turn in late for work.

- Don't yell at your kids when they struggle with their homework or other chores.

- Leave thank you notes for your loved ones.

These may seem like tiny gestures right now, and they are, but the ripple effect they create is extraordinary. Once you do an act of kindness, you don't just brighten someone else's day; you also inspire them to be kind to others.

So, one act of compassion serves as a trigger for a series of many other acts, one leading to another. In this manner, the kindness ripple keeps growing bigger and touches many hearts in the process to spread warmth all around.

So far, we have discussed many aspects of gratitude. Now, I'll tackle an important aspect often considered the heart of one's life: the relationships you have in your life.

Let us look at how you can use the power of gratitude to strengthen your bond with loved ones and manifest happiness all around you.

"It's not happiness that brings us gratitude.
It's gratitude that brings us happiness."

Jeremiah Say

Gratitude is one of the **strongest** and most **transformative** states of being. It shifts your **perspective** from lack to abundance and allows you to focus on the good in your life, which in turn pulls more **goodness** into your reality.

— **Jen Sincero**, bestselling author of *You Are a Bad Ass*

Section 7

Gratitude and Relationships

"Thankfulness is the beginning of gratitude. Gratitude is the completion of thankfulness. Thankfulness may consist merely of words. Gratitude is shown in acts."

Henri Frederic Amiel

Introduction to Section 7: Gratitude and Relationships

You need both kind words and loving gestures to build and grow relationships. Relationships thrive on trust, love, respect, equality, sincerity, and lots of warmth.

All of this is only possible when you value the other person and acknowledge his/her presence and efforts in your life and relationship. All relationships, whether with your partner, kids, siblings, parents, cousins, co-workers, bosses, vendors, friends, neighbors, social networks, and absolutely anyone you wish to form a relationship with, need this.

One of the key benefits of gratitude that I talked about earlier in this book was its ability to make hearts grow fonder. Compared to those who don't create any space for gratitude in their lives, people who appreciate and acknowledge each other in relationships tend to have stronger bonds and healthier relationships that last.

Similarly, if you feel concerned about the eerie distance that has somehow crept in between you and your spouse, disconnected from your kids, or the strain you feel in your bond with your parents, it is time to bring gratitude into the equation. Trust me, it works like a magic wand at times. With a simple swish and flick, gratitude restores harmony in any chaotic and dull relationship.

This section focuses on this aspect, giving you guidance on how to use gratitude to mend broken bonds and make your life an absolute treasure to enjoy.

Chapter 21: Gratitude for Your Partner

"It's not where you're in your life; it's who you have by your side that matters."

Anonymous

With loved ones by your side, even the thorns along the journey seem bearable. The thorns sting you, yes, but with your dear ones constantly holding your hand, the pain subsides.

Let us learn how to make these relationships more beautiful with gratitude, starting with cultivating gratitude for your partner.

Gratitude for Your Partner/Spouse

Being in love is a great feeling. Having someone with whom to spend the rest of your life and with whom to share many beautiful and even unexpected or undesirable moments of your life is beautiful.

However, at times, the partnership goes through a rough patch. Conflicts and disagreements build up, slowly taking away the spark that once created a magnificent fire in your relationship.

Usually, this boils down to a lack of appreciation and gratitude for one another. Whether it's two people dating or something more serious like a marriage, when partners in an intimate relationship stop acknowledging each other, things tend to go downhill fast.

If you are going through a rocky phase with your partner, or you want to makes your bond stronger and more passionate, start using gratitude as a tool to make things better.

- Every morning, tell your partner how much you love him/her. If the two of you are currently miles apart, leaving a text message would suffice.

- At least once during the day, appreciate any one of your partner's gestures and efforts in the relationship. For example, you could thank your partner for being with you through difficult times or understanding your preoccupation with an important work project.

- Send a surprise gift to his/her workplace every once in a while. Flowers, chocolates, food, or even a sweet 'thank you' card can easily do the trick to make him/her feel special.

- When the two of you are together, make the time count by giving each other special attention.

- Instead of staying glued to your phone or laptop, spend time talking to each other and doing things the two of you love. Gratitude does not always have to be an explicit "thank you" or "I love you." Being with each other and engaging in activities that bring you both joy is also good enough to show your partner how much he/she means to you.

- Whenever your partner does something sweet for you, say, make you breakfast, drop by at lunchtime to your workplace so the two of you can have time together, or does something nice for your family, let him/her know how much you appreciate that.

- Admire your partner and tell him/her how beautiful/handsome she/he is. Appreciating your partner's looks, style, behavior, etc., is a great way to make your partner feel loved.

Start working on these strategies, and in a matter of a few days, you will have reignited the spark that was slightly extinguishing.

If you have kids, you understand how happier they make your life, which is why it is imperative to express your gratitude to them. Move on to the next chapter to learn how to do that.

"Gratitude can transform common days into thanksgivings, turn routine jobs into joy, and change ordinary opportunities into blessings."
— **William Arthur Ward**

Chapter 22: Gratitude for Your Kids

"Children are the hands by which we take hold of heaven."

Henry Ward Beecher

With kids, life certainly becomes all the more challenging and certainly happier and meaningful too. If you have kids, want to have some kids one day, or have kids in the family, you already know how much color and flavor they add to life and how they teach you something beautiful every day.

Considering that, it is only important to have gratitude for them. If you want your kids to love and respect you and share a close bond with you, one where they can pour their heart out to you, you need to show them they matter.

Here's how you can do that with the help of gratitude.

Be Grateful to Your Kids

It's so unfortunate that many of us think showering kids with lavish gifts and expensive gadgets is the key to their heart; it's not. In reality, it is only quality time spent with them that helps us nourish our bond with them and turn that bond into a lush plant that bears the fruits of love, care, and kindness.

Your kids need you to be around them; they need you to show them that you honor and value them. While you don't need to go overboard with that and spoil them, you surely need to express your love and gratitude towards them.

- Greet your kids with love and joy every morning. Plop a kiss on their head, embrace them and tell them how much you love them.

- For older kids who don't appreciate PDA much, just telling them how good it feels to have them in your life and wishing them a good day is enough.

- If your kids are adults and living separately, you could send them loving messages now and then.

- Appreciate the little efforts your kids make to help you out. If your son placed his sneakers neatly in the shoe rack instead of throwing them on the bedroom floor, give him a pat on the back and appreciate his good manners.

- Let your kids know how beautiful they are. Saying things like, "You are handsome, my boy," or "You are a beautiful girl," or "You are amazing as you are" are great ways to validate them.

- Give your kids occasional presents and not just on their birthdays or festivals. There's no rule that the gifts need not be lavish all the time. Taking your kid to a picnic or getting him a bar of chocolate is enough too.

- Have meals together and offer prayers of gratitude for the food. When you do this as a family, it teaches your kids to be grateful for what they have. Also, show them how to be grateful for everything they have, so they learn it from a tender age.

- When your kid makes a mistake, please don't be too hard on him/her. Instead of penalizing him/her, or admonishing him/her, help him/her understand the consequences of the action and let him/her know it is okay to make mistakes, but even more important to learn from them.

- Spend quality time with your kids daily talking about things they like, asking about their day at school, reading them stories, playing with them, and getting to know them better.

- When your kid talks to you about his/her feelings, listen patiently and don't dismiss them. Instead of asking your boy to be strong if he cries, let him cry and make him feel comforted.

- Leave little notes of "thank you for being a great daughter" or "I love you, my son" in the lunch box.

In a few days of working on these practices, you will find your kids loving and trusting you more, thanks to gratitude. As you strengthen your love with them, pay attention to your relationship with your parents and relatives, too.

"Train yourself never to put off the word or action for the expression of gratitude."

Albert Schweitzer

"Gratitude is a powerful emotion to use for **manifesting** because normally we feel gratitude after we **receive** something. So the **emotional signature** of gratitude means it has already happened."

— **Joe Dispenza**, bestselling author of *Supernatural*

Chapter 23: Gratitude for Parents and Relatives

"Children are our most valuable resource."

Herbert Hoover

I am sure you can relate to feeling what Herbert Hoover says towards your kids. Your parents have the same sentiments for you. They loved you and nurtured you with care and affection when you were young; they made it possible for you to turn into a responsible adult.

Unfortunately, although you love them a lot and they are probably aware of this fact, it is possible to forget to express parental love to your parents, thanks to the hustle and bustle of daily life. Sometimes, even days can go by without speaking to your parents or your favorite aunt.

It is understandable how life gets to us, but it is crucial to acknowledge your loved ones because they make your life brighter.

Gratitude for Your Parents and Relatives

Your parents need you just as you needed them when you were a child. You may not always be physically there for them, but your kinds words can be. Just letting them know how much you miss and care for them is often sufficient to strengthen their spirits.

- If your parents live far off or separately, leave them a loving message once in the morning wishing them a good day followed by an "I love you."

- Before you sign off at night, let your parents know how much you miss them.

- Every few days, share a loving memory you have with them and thank them for giving you a good childhood.

- Appreciate all your parents did for you through messages, calls, and emails.

- Write a detailed gratitude letter to your parents once every 2 to 3 months and send it to them accompanied by a lovely gift.

- Ensure you wish your parents well on their birthdays, special occasions, and holidays.

- Additionally, please drop by to see them whenever possible; it makes all the difference.

- If it is difficult for them to do certain chores, help out as much as possible.

- As for your relatives, leave them compassionate messages and call them up every few weeks to inquire about their well-being.

- You can create a group for your family on Whatsapp or any other social media, so you can all stay connected and share each other's daily whereabouts or special memories.

- Have big family gatherings every once in a while, to catch up with one another, and reminisce beautiful, old memories.

Your life may be great as it is, but once you start following these guidelines, it will become more delightful than ever.

Like family, your friends play a pivotal role in your life, and so do your social networks. You may not always tell them how much they matter to you, but it is time you need to start doing so.

"There are only two ways to live your life. One is as though nothing is a miracle. The other is as though everything is a miracle."

Albert Einstein

Chapter 24: Gratitude for Your Friends and Social Networks

"True friends are never apart, maybe in distance, but never in heart."

Helen Keller

Friends add lots of laughter and adventure to your life. With every friend, you embark on an exciting new journey and create a new bond. I still share a great bond with my childhood friends, and to this day, I have found them to be by my side when I need them the most.

Just like your friends make your routine life joyful, your social network and business contacts add value to your professional life and endeavors. Therefore, to live a well-rounded life where you maintain a healthy, happy relationship with everyone, it is essential to express your gratitude to your friends and contacts.

Be Grateful for Your Friends

Your friends may not expect you to shower them with 'love yous' or 'miss yous' now and then, but they certainly would appreciate it if you showed them how much you value them.

Here are some gratitude-based gestures you can implement to draw your friends nearer to you:

- Set reminders for their birthdays and then send them personalized wishes on their special day.

- Create a group with your close friends so that all of you stay in touch with each other. Every time a friend mentions any special occasion, reach out to him her, send your best wishes, or even show up physically to offer support.

- Call your close friends once every few months to have a detailed talk.

- It is nice to send a detailed "thank you" note along with an appreciation of everything they have done for you every couple of months.

- Surprise your friend with nice presents at least once a year.

- When a friend asks you for any help, and there's no solid reason to excuse yourself from it, be there for him/her.

Whatever you do for your friends will come back to you in the form of lovely gestures from them.

Gratitude for Social Networks and Business Contacts

Whether it's your superiors, subordinates, vendors, business partners, or social network, everyone plays an important role in your professional life. That's why it is important to be thankful to them.

- Thank your boss for all the work and efforts to teach you, and help you grow every few months. You could send them a thank you card with a personalized gift, or just verbally acknowledge their efforts to support you.

- Let your coworkers know how much you acknowledge their support.

- Do nice things for your colleagues every once in a while. For example, take colleagues out for lunch, coffee, or help them with their workload.

- Send personalized gift baskets to your vendors and partners to appreciate their efforts.

- Reach out to your social contacts, thank them for their support whenever you asked for it, and let them know their presence matters in your life.

- efforts to please you and help you grow.

"Be grateful for what you already have while you pursue your goals. If you aren't grateful for what you already have, what makes you think you would be happy with more."

Roy T. Bennett

Give yourself a gift of five minutes of **contemplation in awe** of everything you see around you. Go outside and turn your attention to the many **miracles** around you. This five-minute-a-day regimen of **appreciation** and **gratitude** will help you to **focus** your life in awe.

— *Wayne Dier, Motivational Speaker and Bestselling Author*

Conclusion

"The struggle ends where gratitude begins."

Neale Donald Walsh

My life is a living testament to this Neale Donald Walsh quote. Every time I allowed gratitude to enter my life, my problems slowly began vanishing.

Gratitude has now spread its roots so far and wide into my life that I cannot travel a day without dipping into my treasure trove of people, things and events I am grateful for.

Even when the road leads to a dead end, or when you fail, there is gratitude in your failings. I want you to succeed, to live, and to stretch yourself as far as you can to become the best version of who you are meant to be.

This book has taught you how to equip yourself with the magnificent power of gratitude and use it to transform your life for the better. Each of its chapters shares with your insightful guidelines and action strategies to enhance your gratefulness and happiness.

Now, you need to start following them to get real-time results.

The ending of this story is up to you.

How will you practice gratitude today?

Scott Allan

One looks back with **appreciation** to the brilliant teachers, but with gratitude to those who touched our human **feelings**. The curriculum is so much necessary raw material, but **warmth** is the vital element for the growing plant and for the **soul** of the child.

— *Carl Jung*

Turn the page to read a chapter from **Empower Your Thoughts** (Book #1 in the *Empower Your Success* Series).

Reduce Your Worry Habit

If you observe your own thinking and how your mind interacts with the world, you become a passenger on a wild ride through a theme park. You can be a witness to all the noise and mayhem that comes with a polluted mind that won't stay in the moment.

People are constantly dealing with their thoughts that focus on "getting" and "having" and "becoming." We are attached to owning something or attached to becoming something.

When things are not going as planned, your mind flips into worry mode. Worry is always grounded in the fear of the future. Worrisome thoughts are thoughts we give permission to take control of our state of mind. We worry when we lack trust or faith.

If faith is the belief that things will work out, worry is the belief that everything is in danger of falling apart. It won't work out. You could fail. This could happen or that could happen. Your thoughts start to play out the worst-case scenarios of a bad outcome that results in you ending up empty handed, broke, or alone.

Worry is a broken loop of fear. This is a daily struggle with the mind. You want to trust in something bigger than yourself, but you can't. So, how can you fight back against the loop of fear that worry creates? How do you stop worrying about the future "possibilities" and start living?

You'll need to bring yourself back to the present moment. It starts with reframing your situation and life in a positive framework. Are you seeing the world as a scary, frightful place? Are you afraid of waking up and finding yourself homeless one day? Do you think you'll lose your job next week?

Well, all these things could happen—or none of them could happen. The extent to which they happen is up to you. Most of the worst things that will ever happen to you take place in your mind first... and that's it! Think about the grand symphony of chaos that is constantly conducted inside your mind. But you, as the conductor of your thoughts, can choose how and what to think about. Imagine that. You are the master of your own mind. Remind yourself of this fact and take time to observe your thoughts.

We always have ideas, voices and opinions, mixed with conflicting thoughts based on information we are not entirely sure is correct. How do you separate the good from the bad? How can you trust what is real and what is misleading? How do you stay mindful when your mind wants to wander, explore, and create its own reality without permission?

The strategy I use to filter out the thoughts I don't need is a mental discipline that gets you to focus in on just the present moment. As most of your thoughts jump around and can be in the past one minute and the present the next, this form of mental conditioning—also known as **reframing your thinking portal**—works because it turns down the volume on noisy, intrusive thoughts.

Worry is conditioning your thoughts to fear. If you were raised by fearful parents and spent most of your youth surrounded by fearful people, then being a worrier will seem the best course of action. This way, you build up your fears of the future and don't take any action for fear of failing.

Right now, make a list of three areas of your life you consistently worry about. Knowing what your triggers are plays a big part in this. Then, when you think about these areas, what thoughts enter your mind? Common themes are thoughts of scarcity, losing something valuable, failing fast, or being embarrassed if your master plan doesn't work out.

You might have fearful thoughts of money or relationships, worry about losing your job or getting ill. These are all legitimate worries. But worry leads to mental paralysis by default, and without taking positive action, you'll end up doing nothing. This ensures the worry habit sticks with its rotation and sets up a loop to capture your thoughts. You must unravel that loop and dismantle the worry habit.

You can empower your thoughts by feeding empowering messages to your mind. It works like the body. If you eat crap and junk food, you're going to feel like a physical garbage can. The mind is no different. Worrisome thoughts generate anxiety. You only get out of it what you feed into it.

Here is how you can eliminate the worry habit right now and gain control over the triggers that set you off.

Worry Thoughts are Fabrications

Worry is believing in false stories that have not come true. You worry about having no money, and yet, there is no evidence to suggest you will always be broke. Maybe you worry about your health and that you might get sick. Well, you will not be healthy forever, you know that. But you have your health today, don't you? Worrisome thoughts are grounded in future fear, like most things we stress about.

Worry is another form of fear. We create most of our fears. They play out in our minds and take over all common sense. What are you worrying about right now? Is it something now or something supposed to happen later?

When you feed into the worry habit, you reinforce the false stories that will likely never happen.

From now on, feed your mind the good stuff it really wants. Try these affirmations instead:

- "I am not worried about tomorrow because today is perfect. The here and now is what I have."

- "I always worry about losing my job, but this has never happened to me. I am a good employee and the company I work for values its workers. Why would I think it could happen now?"

Break down your worrisome thoughts and expose these demons for what they are: False fabrications that rarely happen. Worry is a habit, and you can break any habit. But you can make your worrisome beliefs come true, too. If you believe that you will be broke, lose your health, or get divorced, then by carrying this worry around with you can manifest it to come true.

Remember: Thoughts have power and can draw toward you the bad as well as the good. If you think you're going to lose your job, you might show up at work acting like someone who doesn't deserve to be there.

Do you think your spouse is going to divorce you? This worry could cause you to become paranoid. Soon you start to track his or her whereabouts until they catch you planting a GPS unit underneath the car. So, while worrisome thinking is grounded in fantasy, you can manifest your worst nightmares to happen by holding onto these worrisome thoughts.

Negative Thinking: Hardwired for Fear

Positive thinking only works if you truly believe the message you're sending to your brain.

There are a few things I want to say about negative thinking. We tend to see negative thinking as something bad that you should be ashamed of. I'll admit that thinking positively and acting in a positive manner is much better than doing things in a negative way. But, it's a philosophy of mine that negative energy is just as important as positive energy.

How can that be?

You must walk through a mile of slimy mud sometimes before you can get to the green grass on the other end. In other words, being negative and experiencing the suffering that goes with it can be a great motivator for making the decision to change.

Negative thinking—or, "living a negative lifestyle", as I like to call it—is a sign that something is not right with your life. Believe it or not, some people seem to enjoy the attention they receive from negative thinking.

If you have an NMA (i.e., Negative Mental Attitude), and you are not happy with this, deciding to switch over to a positive frame of mind requires that you take intentional action to get your momentum moving.

Some of the world's greatest success stories have come from people who lived through hell and decided to change their lives. You can also look at the people who have everything going for them, and yet, they are unhappy, and it shows in their attitude.

I truly believe that living a positive lifestyle has very little to do with how much you own or how successful you are. It comes down to attitude in every aspect of your life. If all it took was money and popularity, then there wouldn't be any misery with people who seemingly have everything.

Thought and Circumstances: How to Attract What You Want

If you are unhappy with your present circumstances, whether it be your job, relationships, or current state of mind, there is only one way to change it: Think differently. I know this sounds like an obvious piece of advice, but there are reasons for this.

Do you know what happens when you think differently? Things on the outside begin to change. Your situation can only change if you do. Here is why.

Your outer world will always reflect the inner. Your success or failure is based on the success and failure going on inside. Succeed in programming your thoughts for having positive experiences and that is what will happen.

People have been known to alter the course of their lives with a shift in attitude. Can you imagine where you would be if you focused everything you had on thinking with a positive attitude? This isn't to say thinking alone will change you, but without it, we can't follow up with positive actions.

What exactly are positive actions? Some examples are: helping people, working toward goals that get you unstuck, streamlining your efforts to make life worth living for yourself and those around.

The circumstances of this life do not control you. While we can't always choose our circumstances, we can decide how to view them. It is just a matter of fact that bad things happen. Life doesn't go according to plan, and it isn't always fun—no matter who you are or how positive your thoughts may be. But you can train yourself in the best way to deal with it.

More Books by Scott Allan

Check out these other bestselling books by Scott Allan. You can visit his website at **www.scottallanauthor.com** to stay up to date on all future book releases, or amazon.com/author/scottallan

Empower Your Thoughts: Control Worry and Anxiety, Develop a Positive Mental Attitude, and Master Your Mindset

Empower Your Fear: Leverage Your Fears To Rise Above Mediocrity and Turn Self-Doubt Into a Confident Plan of Action

Empower Your Success: Success Strategies to Maximize Performance, Take Positive Action, and Engage Your Enthusiasm for Living a Great Life

Rejection Reset: A Strategic Step-By-Step Program for Restoring Self-Confidence, Reshaping an Inferior Mindset, and Thriving In a Shame-Free Lifestyle

Rejection Free: How To Choose Yourself First and Take Charge of Your Life By Confidently Asking For What You Want

Do It Scared: Charge Forward With Confidence, Conquer Resistance, and Break Through Your Limitations

Relaunch Your Life: Break the Cycle of Self-Defeat, Destroy Negative Emotions, and Reclaim Your Personal Power

Drive Your Destiny: Create a Vision for Your Life, Build Better Habits for Wealth and Health, and Unlock Your Inner Greatness

The Discipline of Masters: Destroy Big Obstacles, Master Your Time, Capture Creative Ideas and Become the Leader You Were Born to Be

The Master of Achievement: Conquer Fear and Adversity, Maximize Big Goals, Supercharge Your Success and Develop a Purpose Driven Mindset

Undefeated: Persevere in the Face of Adversity, Master the Art of Never Giving Up, and Always Beat the Odds Stacked Against You

Fail Big: Fail Your Way to Success and Break All the Rules to Get There

Empower Your Success with the Empowerment Series

About Scott Allan

Scott Allan is a bestselling author who has a passion for teaching, building life skills, and inspiring others to take charge of their lives.

Scott's mission is to give people the strategies needed to design the life they want through choice.

He believes successful living is a series of small, consistent actions taken every day to build a thriving lifestyle with intentional purpose.

By taking the necessary steps and eliminating unwanted distractions that keep you stuck, you are free to focus on the essentials.

You can connect with Scott online at:

Website: http://scottallaninternational.com/

Instagram
https://www.instagram.com/scottallanauthor/

Facebook
https://www.facebook.com/scottallanauthor

What Did You Think of
Empower Your Gratitude?

First of all, thank you for purchasing this book *Empower Your Gratitude.* I know you could have picked any number of books to read, but you picked this book and for that I am extremely grateful.

If you enjoyed this book and found some benefit in reading this, I'd like to hear from you and hope that you could take some time to <u>post a review on Amazon</u>.

Your feedback and support will help this author to greatly improve his writing craft for future projects and make this book even better.

All the best,
Scott Allan

Made in the USA
Las Vegas, NV
15 August 2021

28226452R00088